D1445140

SHOULD WE WORRY ABOUT FAMILY CHANGE?

HQ518 .L48 2003

Lewis, Jane (Jane E.)
0134167322759
Should we worry about
 family change? /
     c2003.

                              2005 01 06

$43.00

GEORGIAN COLLEGE LIBRARY 2002

Should We Worry about Family Change?

The 2001 Joanne Goodman Lectures

JANE LEWIS

250201

LEARNING RESOURCE CENTRE
Georgian College
825 Memorial Avenue
Orillia, Ontario   L3V 6S2

UNIVERSITY OF TORONTO PRESS
Toronto Buffalo London

© University of Toronto Press Incorporated 2003
Toronto Buffalo London
Printed in Canada

ISBN 0-8020-8746-9

Printed on acid-free paper

National Library of Canada Cataloguing in Publication

Lewis, Jane (Jane E.)
   Should we worry about family change? / Jane Lewis.

   (Joanne Goodman lectures ; 2001)
   Includes bibliographical references and index.
   ISBN 0-8020-8746-9

   1. Family. 2. Social change. 3. Family policy. I. Title. II. Series.

   HQ518.L48 2003   306.85   C2003-901907-1

University of Toronto Press acknowledges the financial assistance to
its publishing program of the Canada Council for the Arts and the
Ontario Arts Council.

University of Toronto Press acknowledges the financial support for
its publishing activities of the Government of Canada through the
Book Publishing Industry Development Program (BPIDP).

The Joanne Goodman Lecture Series

has been established by Joanne's family

and friends to perpetuate the memory of her

blithe spirit, her quest for knowledge, and

the rewarding years she spent at the

University of Western Ontario.

Contents

Foreword

The Joanne Goodman lectures were established at the University of Western Ontario in 1975 to honour the memory of the elder daughter of the Honourable Edwin A. Goodman and Mrs Goodman of Toronto. Each year the university invites a scholar to deliver three lectures on some aspect of the history of the English-speaking peoples, particularly those of the Atlantic Triangle of Canada, the United Kingdom, and the United States, that will be of interest to members of the university community and the general public. The list of those who have participated over a quarter of a century indicates the distinction of the lectures and the part they play in the intellectual life of this institution and of the whole country. The University of Western Ontario is grateful to Mr Goodman for this generous and moving benefaction, dedicated to a student who loved history and enjoyed her years at the university.

It was a particular pleasure in 2001 to welcome the return of our distinguished alumna Jane Lewis to the university where she earned her PhD in history in 1979. Many faculty members, myself included, have happy memories of her earlier years here. Now Barnett Professor of Social Policy at Oxford University, Jane Lewis began her career at the London School of Economics and Political Science, where she became Professor of Social

Policy in 1991. Before being appointed to her present chair, she was also Professor of the History of Medicine at Oxford University and Professor of Social Policy at Nottingham University. A Fellow of the Royal Society of Canada, the author or editor of two dozen books as well as many articles on social history and social policy, she has been visiting professor at many universities in Europe and other parts of the world. She has also served as an adviser to British and foreign governments and been a member of many investigative bodies. No wonder members of the history department here continue to look with awe and pride on her great achievements.

Neville Thompson
University of Western Ontario

Acknowledgments

This book is based on lectures given in the Department of History at the University of Western Ontario in September 2001 as part of the Joanne Goodman Lecture Series. I was honoured to have been asked to give them and would like to thank the members of the department, especially Professor J.N. Thompson, and the audience for their warm welcome and their comments.

Introduction:

The Decline of the Traditional Male-Breadwinner, Two-Parent Family

IN THEIR CLASSIC 1953 TEXT ON THE FAMILY Burgess and Locke provided a case study of a typical American family from the perspective of a child, as represented in the following excerpt:

My family, consisting of Mother, Father, and myself, has always been very closely knit ... The harmony in our family results from the democratic or companionship relationship. My father is the chief breadwinner of the family; however, all of his decisions are reached only after discussions with Mother. Mother shares in the financial business of the family by keeping and managing the budget. In late years I have shared in the discussions of major importance and have had my part in deciding important questions.

An outsider looking in on us would think that we were a very silly group because of our demonstrations of love for each other ... My father does not show his love for Mother by showering her with gifts ... but rather by sharing all activities with her and spending his spare time with her. Mother is a very affectionate type of person and is always doing minor unnecessary things to add to our comfort and enjoyment. (pp. 189–90)

This passage depicts the traditional family in terms of its stability, firm division of labour between the parents, and reliance on consultation and consensus, if not democracy. 'Mother' may merit a capital letter, but she does not make the decisions. Some fifty years later, there is strong nostalgia for this family form among many politicians and academic commentators. The traditional nuclear family of the 1950s to many represents an ideal: a warm, secure 'haven in a heartless world' (Lasch, 1977), free of the patriarchal domination characteristic of (at least middle-class) families fifty years earlier. The contrast between the traditional 1950s family and the confusing and shifting family structures and practices of the early twenty-first century is huge. Even the meaning of family is no longer certain. Both artificial

reproduction and the increasingly messy nature of intimate relationships mean that the family is no longer 'natural'; biological
and social motherhood and fatherhood can be separated. To
Francis Fukuyama (1999), this traditional 1950s family is part of
a 'world we have lost,' eclipsed by the widespread social
change that he has termed 'the great disruption.'

However, the kind of traditional family described by Burgess
and Locke was the predominant family form for only a relatively brief period. Taking a longer view reveals periods – in the
nineteenth century, for example – when unmarried motherhood
was common (Shorter, 1975; Coontz, 1991). Historically lesbian
and gay relationships have been considerably more fluid and
varied than heterosexual partnerships. But since the 1960s, the
kind of traditional family described by Burgess and Locke has
substantially disappeared, and this trend is the focus of this
book. While a majority of children in Western countries still live
in two-parent families at any one time, a very large number of
children, almost half of the child population in the United
States, can expect to spend some time in a 'non-traditional'
household, either as a result of being born outside marriage, or
as a result of parental divorce. The pattern of activity in the
household – the contributions made by men and women – has
also changed profoundly. Women are now far more likely to
work outside the home, although they continue to do most of
the housework and child care (Gershuny, 2000). Family change
is most obviously manifest in the dramatic changes in family
form, but there have also been fundamental shifts in economic
behaviour and in normative ideas about the family among both
policy makers and the general public.

But, should we care? It was not only the poet Philip Larkin
(1988) who said that our families make us sick. At the end of the
1960s and beginning of the 1970s anthropologists and psycholo-
gists railed against the damage families inflicted (Leach, 1967;
Cooper, 1972), while feminists exposed the darker side of the

power imbalance in families that resulted in poverty for women and children and, at the extreme, in domestic violence (Barrett and McIntosh, 1982). These critics effectively called into question the cosy image of the 'companionate' nuclear family. What went on behind the front door of the family home was largely unknown. But serious family problems have in the past often been acknowledged (although not often addressed by either public or private law). By the late twentieth century 'the Kellogg's Cornflakes packet family' seemed no longer to exist. People were not getting married as much, were cohabiting, were divorcing in droves when they did marry, and were having children outside marriage. Women especially were behaving differently inside intimate relationships, and in recent years the role of full-time housewife/homemaker has come close to extinction. There were always lots of families who did not conform to the Burgess and Locke model, even in its heyday of the 1950s. But the ideal held firm. In the late twentieth century the real shock was not just the dramatic change in people's behaviour, but the apparent lack of any common understanding as to what the family should look like or what its adult male and female members should contribute to it.

This situation is particularly difficult given that the family, rather than the individual, has been regarded as the fundamental unit of modern liberal societies. It was male heads of families who voted and entered into contracts. Women were prohibited from doing either until the late nineteenth and early twentieth centuries in most Western societies. The family based on the married pair has long been viewed as bedrock. Mary Ward, the best-selling Victorian novelist, mounted a ferociously polemical defence of the unreformed British divorce law in the early twentieth century in face of its more relaxed American counterpart on the ground that marriage imposed rational bonds on irrational sexual urges. Furthermore, the married couple was viewed as the *polis* in miniature. If husband and wife could not reach an accommodation, then what chance was there for the wider society? In this view, indissoluble marriage was a discipline and an order, which also meant that it had to be construed as a matter of public interest and not just a private relationship.

The family has been seen as the place in which dependants, young and old, can expect care and nurture, in contrast to the ruthless competition of the public world of politics, business, and employment, where the weak must perforce go to the wall. The separation of spheres between public and private thus served a necessary purpose. The late nineteenth-century social theorist Herbert Spencer (1876) believed that evolutionary progress involved the separation of the family from the public world and the harmonious cooperation of men and women. 'Differences of constitution' between men and women would result in progress towards an 'equal but different' model of separate spheres for the sexes, whereby men engaged in the public world of work and citizenship, and women, in their role as homemakers, provided succour for family members. Spencer would have approved of the picture of the family drawn by Burgess and Locke. Most early twentieth-century authors who wrote on marriage and the family adopted an evolutionary perspective and believed that the conjugal family was the place in which obligation was fulfilled and altruism learned, and, furthermore, that this was fundamentally 'natural.' The basis for these ideas received new impetus at the end of the twentieth century from the 'new biology.'

But the traditional male-breadwinner model family, with its male earner and female housewife/carer, became the norm in theory and in practice. There is considerable evidence that this family form was internalized as an ideal, even among working people, whose reality was often very different. Tilly and Scott (1975) have shown how working-class women were likely to engage in casual employment when necessary, and John Gillis (1997) has pointed out that cohabitation was much more common in early twentieth-century England, following informal marital separation or widowhood, than it was in the middle of the century. Early twentieth-century working-class wives, who were frequently pregnant and who also had to undertake hard household labour, were as likely to support the idea of a gendered division of labour and a 'family wage' as male trade unionists of that time. Women who had to do paid work as well as unpaid work were to be pitied.

The concept of the traditional male-breadwinner model family was also firmly embedded in private law and public policy. The laws of marriage and divorce not only regulated entry into marriage and exit from it, but also effectively prescribed a particular idea of marriage. First and foremost, sex was to be kept inside marriage. Second, family law underpinned traditional notions of obligation between men and women. The idea that marriage involves male financial support for women and children, and female performance of domestic and caring duties – the essence of the traditional male-breadwinner model – was reflected in what happened when marriage ended under the old fault-based divorce laws (Weitzman, 1981, 1985). The courts allocated blame and made decisions about children (who invariably went with their mothers), property (which for most part stayed with the husband), and alimony (for the dependent wife).

Assumptions about the male-breadwinner model were also embedded in public policy and systems of social support that grew up in virtually all Western countries during the early part of the twentieth century. Modern states are by definition also welfare states, although they vary considerably in regard to extent to which collective provision has been institutionalized. The settlement at the heart of the modern welfare state is that between capital and labour. But it has increasingly been recognized that this settlement entailed a particular kind of gender regime. The traditional labour contract, hammered out in the early part of the twentieth century through restrictions on the hours of work, minimum wage regulations, pension entitlements, sickness and unemployment insurance, and paid holidays was designed first and foremost for the regularly employed male breadwinner, and provision had to be made for women and children, again classified as dependants.

The gender settlement meant that those marginal to the labour market got financial support via dependants' benefits. Alain Supiot (1999) has described the labour/capital settlement in terms of security traded for dependence. A similar set of arrangements can be said to have marked the gender settlement. The male-breadwinner model was based on a set of assumptions about male and female contributions at the household level, with men having the primary responsibility to earn and women having the primary responsibility to care for the young and the old. Female economic dependence was inscribed in the model. Sir William Beveridge's blueprint for the postwar welfare state in the United Kingdom (Cmd 6404, 1942) gave an enthusiastic welcome to the equal-but-different parts to be played by men and women in the family. He insisted on using the term 'partnership' to describe marriage and drew attention to the importance of women's role in reproduction at a time when low birth rates were a particular cause for concern. In the postwar welfare settlement, married women were to pay less by way of social insurance contributions and receive less by way of benefits. To this day, tax/benefit systems are rarely fully 'individualized'; the unit of assessment is often the couple or the household.

By mid-century, then, the male-breadwinner model was built into the fabric of society, and the postwar welfare settlement assumed regular and full male employment *and* stable families in which women would be provided for largely via their husbands' earnings and social insurance contributions. When this is understood, the amount of material as well as psychic investment in the traditional family model becomes clearer and the anxiety over its apparent demise easier to understand. The traditional two-parent nuclear family was understood as fundamental to the success of Western economies. The classic sociology of the family published in the immediate postwar decades tried to explain family change in the context of societal change, and together with neoclassical economic theory, argued that the stable, traditionally organized two-parent nuclear family was supremely well-suited to producing individuals able to function in a liberal, individualist market economy.

The traditional family was also assumed to be natural. Biological essentialism was as prevalent in the mid-twentieth-century sociological and economic analyses of the family as it was in the work of Herbert Spencer. Burgess and Locke's adult family members were portrayed as *choosing* to live as they did, but the traditional family was also presented as the only legitimate alternative. The neoclassical economists explained why this was so. As rational economic actors, men and women chose to marry in order to maximize the gains that followed from a traditional division of labour. Thus women chose men who would be good providers and men chose women who would be good homemakers and mothers (Becker, 1981).

The notion that the traditional family was both the most efficient way of meeting the needs of the modern public world and that it was the most 'natural' family form was pervasive. The male-breadwinner family was accepted as the conventional family form. Other forms were stigmatized; families affected by divorce and unmarried motherhood heavily so in most Western countries until the 1970s, but also families in which wives went out to work (until the 1960s), and those in which mothers with small children worked (until the late 1980s).

The traditional family, then, has been seen as bedrock. And yet anxiety over its fragility is far from new. In 1906, Helen Bosanquet, a pillar of the British Charity Organization Society, clearly described the characteristics of the stable family in her book entitled *The Family* ('family' was capitalized throughout the text). It required the firm authority of the father and cooperative industry of all its members. Bosanquet made the connection between the traditional male-breadwinner family form and its national importance in maintaining male work incentives: 'Nothing but the combined rights and responsibilities of family life will ever rouse the average man to his full degree of efficiency and induce him to continue working after he has earned sufficient to meet his own personal needs ... The Family, in short, is from this point of view the only known way of ensuring with an approach to success that one generation will exert itself in the interests and for the sake of another' (p. 222). She believed that the stable family sheltered young and old through one strong bond of mutual helpfulness (making old-age pensions, then under discussion, superfluous), and rendered the development of 'a residuum' (what today would be termed an 'underclass') impossible, by training the young in the habits of labour and obedience. Traditional families thus provided work incentives for men as well as a sphere for the socialization of children. Those involved in social action in the period before the First World War tried to inculcate orderly habits in the homes of the poor, via voluntary visiting, personal social work, and settlement houses (Lewis, 1991; Sklar, 1995; Ginzberg, 1990). Bosanquet made the point that there were families at both ends of the social scale who failed to conform to the ideal family form and behaviour. However, anxiety on the part of social commentators and politicians was confined to poor families, who stood to become burdens on the state if things went wrong.

This anxiety about 'family responsibility' is fundamental and continued throughout the twentieth century, although mid-century probably marked the period of greatest optimism on the part of commentators about the capacity of families to maintain themselves and to support their members effectively. Men and women had rallied to the war effort and could surely be counted on to cooperate with the new structures of social provision that characterized the postwar settlement in most Western countries. However, by the 1980s the pace of change in family form and practices had given rise to anxieties that far outstripped those of Bosanquet and her fellow social commentators. At a time when New Right governments were determined to roll back the state, it was crucial that the family could be counted on to bear its responsibilities for supporting young and old. In the United Kingdom, the first Thatcher administration made this explicit in a White Paper entitled 'Growing Older': 'Whatever level of public expenditure proves practicable, and however it is distributed, the primary sources of support and care for elderly people are informal and voluntary. These spring from the personal ties of kinship, friendship, and neighbourhood. They are irreplaceable. It is the role of public authorities to sustain and, where necessary, develop – but never to displace – such support and care. Care in the community must increasingly mean care by the community' (Cmnd. 8173, 1982). The fear was that family responsibility had increasingly been subverted by state provision. With high levels of divorce, for example, what were the chances of the family caring for its elderly dependent members? Were 'blended families' likely to result in more possible carers for elderly parents or fewer? And were women in their fifties, who were increasingly likely to be in the labour market, going to be able and willing to care?

These remain issues of concern. Indeed they have become more serious as Western populations continue to age. Also central to the debate were increasing numbers of lone mothers and their effect on the educational achievement, behaviour, and, eventually, family formation of their children. During the 1950s and 1960s, British and American psychological, sociological, and medical research concluded that marital conflict was as bad for a child as divorce (Goode, 1956), and that divorce might actually be better for children than living with unhappy parents who were effectively 'emotionally divorced' (Despert, 1953; Nye, 1957). But by the 1980s social research was emphasizing the bad effects of 'family breakdown' on children.

The concern about family change is mainly about whether the family will be able to take responsibility – in terms of both financial support and care – for its members. But it is also about the maintenance of order. Fukuyama (1999) considered the steep rise in juvenile crime to be part of the 'great disruption.' The irresponsible behaviour of young men who do not do military service, and who are not tied into families, is increasingly feared, especially if the men are black. Bosanquet doubted the work ethic of young men at the beginning of the twentieth century, and almost a hundred years later, George Gilder (1987) in the United States and Geoff Dench (1994) in the United Kingdom have worried about them as absent fathers and as what Charles Booth (1892) would have termed 'semi-criminal and vicious' members of society. Booth's 'submerged tenth' lives on in Charles Murray's 'underclass.'

The deep-seated concern over the family at the turn of the twenty-first century is both moral and social. Family change on the scale that we have seen and are seeing smacks of moral decay. Are we looking into the abyss where we will no longer care for our kin and learn the habits of industry and of respect for others? That is the often unspoken fear. Some cross-national studies suggest that we are indeed becoming more 'individualistic' in the West (Inglehart, 1997). However, many studies tell us that we still attach enormous value to family life (e.g., Scott, 1997).

Family change is very complicated. It is not necessarily a cause for 'worry,' although most academic and political commentators would, I think, be prepared to say that the pace of change warrants careful attention. What to *do* in face of such change is more contentious still. For the most part the nostalgia for the traditional family has not translated into firm policies designed to put the clock back, for example by returning working mothers to the home, or by making divorce much harder to obtain. Indeed, at least in the English-speaking countries, politicians on the right, who are most likely to wax eloquent on the subject of family values, are also usually the most loath to accept state intervention in the family. Thus American commentators of the early 1980s asked: 'Will society return control of children to the family ... Can we return self assurance to mothers and fathers, along with confidence in how they raise their young? Or is it too late to stop the inexorable movement led by professionals, justified by academics and funded by the Government and publicised by the media, that claims society knows best – and is ready to tell mothers and fathers how to do it, and even to do it for them?' (Berger and Berger, 1983).

Similarly, Ferdinand Mount (1983), Mrs Thatcher's family policy adviser during the same period, described the family as having been in 'permanent revolution' against the unwanted intrusions of the state. Left-leaning commentators and some feminist writers, particularly in the United States, have also expressed distrust of government intervention. Thus, Christopher Lasch (1977) has argued that the family, as a sanctuary from the public world, has been invaded and subjected to outside control through 'the agency of management, bureaucracy, and professionalization,' and Jean Bekthe Elshtain (1981) has argued strongly in favour of 'family privacy.' But the historical evidence suggests that while men and women, especially in poor families, have expressed distaste for the terms, conditions, and methods of assistance offered to them, they have not said that they want no help at all. Indeed, Pat Thane (1984) has argued that working-class men and women in the early part of the twentieth-century wanted non-stigmatizing and nonintrusive help to tide them over in hard times. What has tended to happen instead, again in the English-speaking countries, is that the divide between public and private worlds has been carefully guarded until the manifestations of family failure become too severe to be ignored – for example, in the form of child abuse – and then government intervention has been unequivocal. The suspicion surrounding state intervention in the family does not suggest that the state has had no interest in the family, merely that it has tended to act negatively rather than positively.

In the chapters that follow I explore, first, the nature of family change in terms of family form and the contributions that men and women make to families; second, the debates about these changes, and the way in which they have been interpreted; and third, what might be done under private law and public policy. My focus is on the relationships between men and women as fathers and mothers, between children and the state, and on the issue of responsibility. The importance of family privacy is not to be dismissed, but it may be possible to promote family responsibility by state intervention that is designed to enable rather than merely to deter, contain, or punish. On this, we need to look beyond the English-speaking world.

1

Behavioural Change

THE TRADITIONAL FAMILY FORM has changed in two key respects: the pattern of women's and, to a lesser extent, men's contribution to the family in regard to both financial support and care, and the structure of the family itself. In both respects there are signs of increasing 'individualization.' Indeed, as I shall argue in Chapter 3, it is tempting for policy makers to conclude that, given the changes in family structure that have produced more single-person and lone-mother households, and given the increase in female labour-market participation, all adults – male and female – should be encouraged to be self-sufficient. In other words, the appropriate model for policy making in respect of labour markets and social protection should be an 'adult worker' rather than a 'male breadwinner.'

However, we should be cautious about how we approach family change. It has become tempting to write about the 'end of marriage' in recent years. There has been a rapid decline in the numbers marrying, and a huge rise in the numbers divorcing and in the proportion of children being born outside marriage. Cohabitation has become much more prevalent. Profound demographic change has taken place over the space of one generation. The 'facts' of family change in these respects are obvious, but the meanings of the changes raise more difficult questions. In regard to labour market change the picture is more equivocal still. Nowhere is there a fully-fledged adult worker model in the sense of equal male and female labour market participation. This means that while women do contribute more cash to households than was the case in the mid-twentieth century, they rarely contribute as much as men. However, women continue to provide the bulk of unpaid care work. Changes in the division of labour between the sexes have been somewhat less dramatic than the changes in family structure.

Changes in Family Structure

The archetypal 'Kellogg's Cornflake packet family' was com-

TABLE 1
Total Fertility Rate per Woman

	1970–75	1995–2000
Australia	2.53	1.79
Canada	1.97	1.55
Denmark	1.97	1.72
Finland	1.62	1.73
France	2.31	1.71
Germany	1.64	1.30
Ireland	3.82	1.90
Italy	2.28	1.20
Netherlands	1.97	1.50
Portugal	2.75	1.37
Spain	2.89	1.15
Sweden	1.89	1.57
UK	2.04	1.72
USA	2.02	1.99

Source: United Nations, 1999, *World Population 1998* (New York: United Nations Publications).

posed of mother and father (who would also be expected to be wife and husband) and two children. Various things have changed regarding this picture. First, the number of children present is much more likely to be smaller, especially in the southern European countries. The one-child and the childless family are increasingly common (see Table 1). The fact that birth rates have fallen most dramatically in the predominantly Roman Catholic countries is surprising. It is extremely difficult to explain changes in fertility, but some observations may be made. In the southern European countries, it seems that birth rates fell as female labour market participation rates increased (see below, Table 12). However, in Sweden both the birth rate and the female labour market participation rate have been high, although birth rates have fallen during the 1990s. It is possible to suggest that, during the 1980s at least, Swedish women found it easier to combine paid work and family responsibilities than did southern European women. Indeed, the dramatic decline in southern European fertility has been attributed in large measure to the difficulties that women experience in this respect. Esping Andersen (2000) has suggested that 'the low fertility equilibrium' is a means of dealing with competing work and family pressures when the state has done very little to help reconcile them. But this leaves the fall in Sweden's birth rate during the 1990s to be explained. This decline may well be related to the greater insecurities in the labour market. With rising unemployment in the early 1990s and greater labour market flexibility, women may have become reluctant to risk taking time off to have children. However, these lines of explanation do not seem to apply to the English-speaking countries very well. Here, female labour market participation rates tend to be high (see below, Table 12) and birth rates are also higher than in many continental European countries, and yet governments have historically done very little to help reconcile work and family responsibilities. Labour markets also tend to be flexible and therefore insecure. In the United Kingdom, as in the United States, there is a high rate of young motherhood, married and unmarried. Indeed, as Coleman and Chandola (1999) have pointed out, without its persistently high teenage birth rate (Table 2), which, unlike the trend in the United States did not show signs of decline in the 1990s, the United Kingdom would look much more like its European neighbours in terms of its fertility rate. Given that the British government has stated that it wishes to reduce the teenage birth rate by 50 per cent, it may also come to face the issue of a low birth rate (and the associated debates over immigration that are taking place in continental Europe). As it is, the UK Office of National Statistics' projections indicate that of all women born in 1972, almost a quarter (23 per cent) will remain childless at age 45.

Men are also more likely to be absent from the family, or to be there as cohabiting partners rather than as husbands. Akerloff

TABLE 2
Births per 1,000 Teenage Women

	1970[1]	1990–95[2]
Australia	50.9	21.0
Canada	42.1	25.0
Denmark	32.4	11.0
Finland	32.2	14.0
France	26.4	12.0
Germany	35.9[3]	17.0
Ireland	16.9	15.0
Italy	42.8[4]	10.0
Netherlands	22.6	6.0
Portugal	29.4[5]	27.0
Spain	14.1	15.0
Sweden	34.0	13.0
UK	49.7	34.0
USA	69.2	58.0

[1]1970 data: Births per 1000 women age 15–19.
[2]1990–1995 data: Births per 1000 women age 15–19.
[3]Data are for West Germany only.
[4]Data are for 1969.
[5]Data are for 1971.

Sources: For 1970 data: United Nations, 1988, *Compendium of Statistics and Indicators on the Situation of Women 1986* (New York: United Nations Publications; for 1990–95 data: United Nations, 1995, *The World's Women, 1995: Trends and Statistics* (New York: United Nations Publications).

(1998) has pointed out that the proportion of US men age 25–34 in families declined from 66 to 40 per cent over the period since 1968. Either they were leaving their families or not marrying in the first place. The problem of 'male flight' has been a common subject for discussion among feminists and conservative politicians.

The most controversial outcome of changes in family structure has been the rise in the proportion of one-parent families,

TABLE 3
Changes in Family Structure in Selected Industrialized Countries, 1960 and 1988 (percentage of family
households that are single-parent)

	1960	1988
Canada	9	15
Denmark	17	20
France	9	12
Germany	8	14
Netherlands	9	15
Sweden	9	13
UK	6	13
USA	9	23

Source: International Labour Organization, 2000,
World Labour Report 2000 (Geneva: International
Labour Organization).

the vast majority of which are headed by lone mothers. Recent
comparable data on lone-parent families are notoriously difficult to obtain, but Table 3 gives some indication as to the pace of
change between the 1960s and the 1980s.

Nevertheless, the picture looks very different depending on
how the data are presented. Table 4, which shows the proportion of children in lone-parent families, looks considerably more
dramatic than Table 5, which shows lone-parent data alongside
that for couple families. Table 6 shows that the increase in the
proportion of one-person households, composed of course of
both young and increasing numbers of elderly people, is as dramatic as the increase in lone-parent families. In the United
States, just over 60 per cent of all children lived with their biological parents throughout the 1990s, and the 2000 statistics
showed a slight drop in the proportion of dependent children
living with lone mothers. Nevertheless, the share of households
made up of two parents and their children – the traditional fam-

TABLE 4
Proportion of Dependent Children Living in Lone-
Parent Families

	1983	1996
Finland	–	15
France	9	13
Germany	–	12
Ireland	5	11
Italy	7	10
Netherlands	8	9
Portugal	–	11
Spain	–	7
UK	11	23
USA	18[1]	23[2]
Canada	–	19

[1]Per cent of children living with lone mother in 1980
(Source: US Census Bureau, 2000).
[2]Per cent of children living with lone mother in 1995
(Source: US Census Bureau, 2000).

Sources: Eurostat, 2000, *The Social Situation in the European Union* (Luxembourg: Office of Publications for the European Communities; US Census Bureau, 2000. *Statistical Abstract of the United States* (Washington: US Census Bureau); Statistics Canada, 1997, '1996 Census: Marital Status, Common-Law Unions and Families,' *The Daily*, 14 Oct. 1997.

ily – fell from 45 per cent in 1960 to just below a quarter (23.5 per cent) for the first time in 2000.

The pathways into lone motherhood are various and have changed over time, which has affected how lone motherhood has been perceived. In the United Kingdom, the proportion of lone mothers was as large at the beginning of the twentieth century as it was in the 1970s, but then, as in other countries, the main cause was widowhood. Now the main causes are divorce, unmarried motherhood, and the breakdown of cohabitation, all

TABLE 5
Per Cent Distribution of Families by Couples and Lone Parents

	Year	Lone-parent families	Couple families
Australia	1996	9.9	89.1
Canada	1996	14.5	85.5
Denmark	1999	8.3	91.7
Finland	1998	13.5	86.5
France	1998	6.2	93.8
Germany	1998	11.6	88.4
Ireland	1996	15.8	84.2
Italy	1998	11.0	89.0
Netherlands	1997	7.6	92.4
Spain	1995	9.6	90.4
Sweden	1997	11.6	88.4
UK	1997	16.0	84.0
USA	1998	14.9	85.1

Source: United Nations, 2000, data from *UN/ECE Database* based on national sources in *Women and Men in Europe and North America – 2000* (New York: United Nations Publications); Australian Bureau of Statistics, 2000, *Australia Social Trends 1999* (Belconnen: Australian Bureau of Statistics).

of which may (especially in the English-speaking countries) be considered moral as well as social problems.

Divorce rates began to rise in most Western countries, but particularly in the English-speaking world during the 1970s, as no-fault divorce legislation was introduced and as access to legal services improved (Table 7) (Phillips, 1988). In addition, remarriage rates have been considerably lower for women, who have been more likely to gain custody of children, than for men. In the United Kingdom the divorce rate increased threefold and the rate of unmarried motherhood increased fourfold in one generation. Divorce is high and stable in northern Europe, with more moderate rates in continental western Europe and low rates in the south, albeit with rising rates of marital separation. The divorce rate in the United Kingdom is higher than in Can-

TABLE 6
One-Person Households (as a percentage of all households)

	1970	1995–98
Australia	14	24
Canada	13	23[1]
Denmark	22	37
Finland	24	35
France	20	30
Germany	31[2]	35
Ireland	13	23
Italy	13	23
Netherlands	17	32
Portugal	10	14
Spain	7	13
Sweden	25	40[1]
UK	18	28
USA	17	25

[1]Data from 1990/3
[2]Data from 1981 (Source Eurostat 1997).

Source: United Nations, 2000, *The World's Women, 2000: Trends and Statistics* (New York: United Nations Publications); Eurostat 1997, *Eurostat Yearbook 1986–1996* (Luxembourg: Office of Official Publications of the European Union).

ada, but lower than in the United States, and has recently begun to fall slightly, but this has much to do with the fact that many fewer people have been getting married (Table 8).

There have been extraordinary rises in the proportion of live births outside marriage in northern Europe, wide variations in the increase in the continental western European countries (high in France, low in Germany), and wide variations in southern European countries (Portugal had a higher rate than many northern countries as early as 1960 and a higher rate than Germany in 1995) (Table 9). Unmarried motherhood, especially

TABLE 7
Crude Divorce Rates, 1973–98 (per 1000 mid-year population)

	1973	1985	1994	1996	1997	1998
Australia	1.21	2.52	2.71	2.87	2.8	2.7
Canada	1.66	2.46	2.72	2.41	2.25	2.28
Denmark	2.52	2.81	2.63	2.43	2.42	2.48
Finland	1.89	1.85	2.70	2.69	2.63	2.67*
France	0.98	1.95	2.00	2.01	2.1	2.00
Germany	1.46[1]	2.10[1]	2.04	2.14	2.29	2.30
Ireland[2]	–	–	–	–	–	–
Italy	0.33	0.27	0.48	0.60	0.60	0.60
Netherlands	1.33	2.35	2.35	2.25	2.16	2.10
Portugal	0.07	0.88	1.24	1.42	1.42	1.50
Spain[2]	–	–	0.81	0.83	0.87	0.90
Sweden	2.00	2.37	2.53	2.42	2.37	2.30
UK	2.14	3.08	2.97	2.91	2.70	2.70
USA	4.36	4.95	4.57	4.33	4.34	4.20

*Provisional data
– Data not available for this year
[1]Data for West Germany only
[2]Ireland passed divorce legislation in 1996 and Spain in 1981.

Sources: Data for 1985: United Nations, 1991, *Demographic Yearbook 1989* (New York: United Nations Publications). Data for 1973: United Nations, 1978, *Demographic Yearbook 1977* (New York: United Nations Publications). Data for 1994 to 1998: United Nations, 2000, *Demographic Yearbook 1998* (New York: United Nations Publications).
Other sources: Council of Europe, 2000, *Recent Demographic Developments in Europe*, 1999. Strasbourg: Council of Europe Publishing; Eurostat, 2000, *European Social Statistics: Demography* (Luxembourg: Office of Publications for the European Communities); US Department of Health and Human Services, 2000, *Monthly Vital Statistics Report*, vol. 47, no. 21; Australian Bureau of Statistics, 2000, *Australian Demographic Trends* (Belconnen: Australian Bureau of Statistics); Statistics Canada, 1998, *Annual Demographic Statistics 1998*, Catalogue 91-213-XPB (Ottawa: Statistics Canada); Statistics Canada, 2000, 'Divorces,' *The Daily*, 28 Sept. 2000.

among young women, is much more prevalent in the English-speaking countries, which has prompted much debate about causes. These are as various as the decline of stigma; the nature of opportunities open to poor young women in countries such as the United Kingdom and the United States, which are prone to greater social inequalities than continental European countries; and the role of state transfers in making such behaviour possible (see Chapter 2).

Table 10 shows marital and extramarital birth rates over a longer period of time for one country, the United Kingdom. These data help to explain why there has been such concern about the high rate of extramarital births at the end of the twentieth century. There has, after all, been a high out-of-wedlock birth rate before (Shorter, 1975). The period of the Second World War is a good example, but during these years, the extramarital rate increased mainly because of marriages that were planned but which did not take place owing to conscription, wartime disruption, and death. There was a significant increase again in the 1960s, when sexual activity among the young increased and sex became increasingly separated from marriage. However, increased sexual activity resulted in a rise in both the extramarital and marital birth rate. This pattern allowed observers to remain sanguine about family change (the divorce rate was still relatively low). In 1969, of extramarital conceptions, 55 per cent were legitimized by marriage, 32 per cent resulted in extramarital births and 14 per cent were aborted (the abortion law was relaxed in the United Kingdom in 1967). Thus, despite the fact that sex and marriage were becoming separated, it was still the case that the majority of those getting pregnant premaritally would have had what were termed 'shot-gun marriages.' It therefore appeared that people were continuing to respect the traditional family form. Of course it is likely that many of those having shot-gun marriages later divorced and entered the statistics of lone motherhood that way (Kiernan, Land, and Lewis, 1998).

TABLE 8
Crude Marriage Rates, 1973–98 (per 1000 mid-year population)

	1973	1985	1994	1996	1997	1998
Australia	8.40	11.20	6.20	5.80	5.80	5.90*
Canada	9.00	7.30	5.50	5.30	5.10	5.10
Denmark	6.10	5.70	6.80	6.80	6.50	6.50*
Finland	7.50	5.30	5.90	4.80	4.60	4.50*
France	7.70	4.90	4.40	4.80	4.90*	4.80*
Germany	6.40[1]	6.00[1]	5.40	5.20	5.20	5.10*
Ireland	7.50	5.30	4.60	4.50	4.30	4.90
Italy	7.60	5.20	5.10	4.90	4.70	4.80
Netherlands	8.00	5.70	5.40	5.50	5.40	5.50
Portugal	9.90	6.70	6.60	6.40	6.60	6.70*
Spain	7.70	5.00	5.00	4.90	4.9	5.10
Sweden	4.70	4.60	3.90	3.80	3.80	3.50*
UK	8.20	6.90	5.70	5.40	5.30	5.10
USA	17.10	10.10	9.10	8.80	8.90	8.4

*Provisional data
– Data not available for this year
[1]Data for West Germany only

Sources: Data for 1985: United Nations, 1991, *Demographic Yearbook 1989* (New York: United Nations Publications). Data for 1973: United Nations, 1978, *Demographic Yearbook 1977* (New York: United Nations Publications). Data for 1994 to 1998: United Nations, 2000, *Demographic Yearbook 1998* (New York: United Nations Publications).
Other sources: Council of Europe, 2000, *Recent Demographic Developments in Europe 2000* (Strasbourg: Council of Europe Publishing); Statistics Canada, 1998, *Annual Demographic Statistics*, Statistics Canada Catalogue 91-213-XPB; US Department of Health and Human Services, 2000, *Monthly Vital Statistics Report*, vol. 43, no. 12 supplement; Statistics Canada, 2001, 'Marriages,' *The Daily*, 15 Nov. 2001.

But in the late twentieth century even this semblance of propriety was increasingly ignored as marriage became separated from parenthood. Fewer non-married pregnant women married before the birth of their babies. Thus, as Table 10 shows, in the 1980s and 1990s, while the extramarital birth rate increased

TABLE 9
Extramarital Birth Rates, 1988–98 (as a percentage of all births)

	1988	1994	1998
Australia	17	26	29
Canada	22	30	31[1]
Denmark	45	47	45[2]
Finland	21	31	37
France	26	36	40*
Germany	16	15	20
Ireland	12	21	28
Italy	6	8	9
Netherlands	10	14	21
Portugal	14	18	20
Spain	9	11	15
Sweden	51	52	55
UK	25	32	38
USA	26	31[3]	33[4]

*Provisional data.
[1]Data for 1996.
[2]Data for 1997.
[3]Data for 1993.
[4]Data from 1999.

Sources: Eurostat, 2000, *Eurostat Yearbook: A Statistical Eye on Europe 1988–1998* (Luxembourg: Office of Official Publications for the European Community); Australian Bureau of Statistics, 2000, *Australian Demographic Trends* (Belconnen: Australian Bureau of Statistics); US Department of Health and Human Service, *National Vital Statistics Report*, vol. 49, no. 5, 24 July 2001; Council of Europe, 2000, *Recent Demographic Developments in Europe*, 2000 (Strasbourg: Council of Europe Publishing).

rapidly, the marital birth rate fell. This development has provoked anxiety among policy makers and politicians.

Cohabitation is the driver of much of the change; it is now a prelude and an alternative to marriage and has contributed to the increasing separation of marriage and parenthood, which

TABLE 10
Marital and Extramarital Births per 1,000 Women Ages 15–44, United Kingdom, 1940–95

	Marital birth rate per 1,000 married women	Extramarital birth rate per 1,000 single, divorced, and widowed women
1940	98.8	5.9
1945	103.9	16.1
1950	108.6	10.2
1955	103.7	10.3
1960	120.8	14.7
1965	126.9	21.2
1970	113.5	21.5
1975	85.5	17.4
1980	92.2	19.6
1985	87.8	26.7
1990	86.7	38.9
1995	82.7	39.6

Sources: Office of Population Censuses and Surveys (OPCS), 1987, *Birth Statistics: Historical Series 1837–1983*, Table 3.2b & c, Series FM1 No. 13 (London: HMSO); OPCS, 1995, *Birth Statistics: Historical Series 1837–1983*, Table 3.1, Series FM1 No. 22 (London: HMSO).

constitutes a more profound shift than the 1960s separation of sex and marriage (Table 11). Cohabitation is still most common as a prelude to marriage. The trend of living together prior to marriage began in the 1970s. By the 1990s in the United Kingdom, 70 per cent of never-married women who married had cohabited with their husbands, compared with 58 per cent of those marrying between 1985 and 1988, 33 per cent of those marrying between 1975 and 1979, and only 6 per cent of those marrying between 1965 and 1969. Cohabiting relationships do seem to be less stable than marriages, four times more so in the United Kingdom according to the British Household Panel data. It seems that increasing numbers of women are opting not to

TABLE 11
Couples Living in Consensual Union as % of All Unions, 1996

	Total	Ages 16–29	% with children*
Australia	9[0]	12[1]	46.0
Canada		46[2]	47.2
Denmark	22	72	40.4
Finland	21	63	39.0
France	14	14	–
Germany	9	40	28.1
Ireland	3	17	40.4
Italy	2	9	40.5
Netherlands	11	46	19.0
Portugal	3	11	–
Spain	2	10	57.0
Sweden	27	73	47.1
UK	9	34	41.7
USA	7[3]	11[4]	

Data from 1995–8.
[0]Data for 1997.
[1]Ages 25–29.
[2]Ages 20–24.
[3]Year 1995. Cohabiting women only.
[4]Ages 20–24. Cohabiting women only. Year 1995.
– Data not available.

Sources: Eurostat, 2000, *The Social Situation in the European Union* (Luxembourg: Office of Publications for the European Union); United Nations, 2000, *The World's Women, 2000: Trends and Statistics* (New York: United Nations Publications); US National Center for Health Statistics, 1997, *Fertility, Family Planning and Women's Health*, Vital Health Statistics Series 23, no. 19; Australian Bureau of Statistics, 1997, *1997 Family Characteristics Survey* (Belconnen: Australian Bureau of Statistics).

marry before they have children and that many of these women are cohabiting. In Canada between 1981 and 1996, there was a 262 per cent increase in cohabitant families with children (Beaujot, 2000, p. 122). The pace of change is such that it is possible to think in terms of the 'rise and fall' of marriage in the twentieth century (Lewis, 2001). Certainly first marriage rates have fallen in most Western countries. In the European Union (EU) in 1998 they were lowest in the United Kingdom.

However, the meaning of cohabitation is far from clear. While most cohabitants do go on to marry, Smock and Gupta (2000) have pointed out that the percentage doing so has declined: from 50 per cent of Canadian unions begun before 1980, to about 30 per cent of unions in the early 1990s. The trend is similar in many other countries, including the United Kingdom, the United States, and France, but not in Germany or the Netherlands (Kiernan, 2000). In the United Kingdom, the probability of cohabitation ending without marriage became greater than the reverse for the first time around 1990 (Murphy, 2000). In the English-speaking countries, cohabitants with children are more likely to be less well off, and Smart and Stevens (2000) have suggested that low-income female cohabitants may well be rational risk takers. Faced with the prospect of living alone with a child or marrying a man with uncertain economic prospects, cohabitation may indeed be the rational course of action. Certainly, British and US data show that an increase in the man's wages makes a couple more likely to marry. In the United States, the dramatic deterioration in the economic position of male manual workers, particularly black men, has been linked to the increase in lone-mother families (Wilson, 1987). The socio-economic characteristics of cohabitants with children are very different in a country such as Sweden, where 53 per cent of women aged 25–27 have their first child in a cohabiting relationship, or France, where the figure is 46 per cent (compared with 17 per cent in the United Kingdom).

Kingsley Davis (1985) offered a series of tests as a means of demonstrating whether marriage was declining: the postponement of marriage, fewer people marrying, a smaller proportion of adult life spent inside marriage, and a rising preference for competing types of intimate relationships. All these tests now seem to indicate that there is indeed a decline in marriage. However, Prinz (1995) developed a model of cohabitation with four stages, in which the fourth and final stage is cohabitation with children. He suggested that at this point cohabitation looks like marriage, but largely because marriage has become more like cohabitation. In fact, it is very difficult to understand the nature of the changes in family structure and thus to assess their significance. All that is certain is that marriage has become a less central unifying cultural experience in Western countries and that the pattern of intimate relationships over the individual life course looks increasingly messy, as people experience multiple cohabitations, marriages, and divorces, and in different sequences. Nor should we forget in all this that the lone individual household is becoming increasingly more common in Western countries. UK data suggest that the fastest growth will be in one-person households over the 2000s (Henley Centre, 1999).

Changing Contributions by Men and Women to the Household

Figure 1 shows the spectrum of gendered patterns of paid work. In western Europe there is evidence of substantial movement away from the male-breadwinner model towards an adult-worker model (Crompton, 1999). However, it is most common to find some form of transitional dual-breadwinner model than a full dual-career model. There may therefore also be convergence between western and eastern European countries, as the latter move in the opposite direction, away from a full dual-career model.

As Table 12 shows, the comparative data on women's postwar labour market participation for Western countries all show an upward trend and men's a downward trend. It is no longer only the Scandinavian countries that have very similar proportions of men and women in the labour market.

FIGURE 1
Patterns of male and female paid work

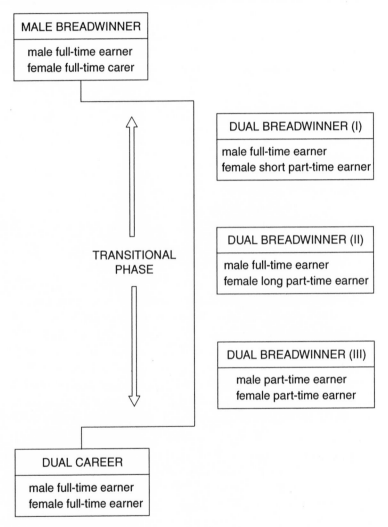

TABLE 12
Labour Force Participation Rates of Population Ages 15–64

	1980 Male	2000 Male	1980 Female	2000 Female
Australia	86.6	83.4	52.0	66.8
Canada	86.0	83.5	57.3	72.1
Denmark	88.3	85.2	71.3	77.3
Finland	79.3	76.7	68.3	72.5
France	81.6	75.7	55.2	62.2
Germany	86.5	81.0	56.2	62.2
Ireland	85.0	79.2	34.7	43.6
Italy	81.9	79.0	39.2	49.9
Netherlands	81.0	79.2	38.2	56.2
Portugal	88.5	82.6	53.4	62.9
Spain	84.5	79.5	32.5	47.9
Sweden	85.4	84.6	69.3	81.6
UK	89.2	83.9	57.0	67.0
USA	83.8	81.5	58.2	70.0

Source: International Labour Organization, 2000, *World Labour Report 2000* (Geneva: International Labour Office).

Since the 1970s Sweden and Denmark have pursued an explicit strategy to draw women into the workforce to deal with the problem of labour market shortage. In other countries the increase in women's paid work has been the result of a complicated mix of supply-side factors – women's desire to work and their increasing economic need to do so – and demand factors. It is noteworthy that in EU countries a very large proportion of the increase in female employment can be accounted for by 'welfare state jobs' in occupations such as teaching and nursing. If we explore the case of three countries – Britain, the Netherlands, and Germany – in which the traditional male-breadwinner model family has been historically well entrenched, at the level of both behavioural and normative expectations, we find that the degree of change has been similar. In the United Kingdom, the British General Household Survey showed that in

1975 81 per cent of men aged 16–64 were economically active compared with only 62 per cent of women. But by 1996 this figure was 70 per cent for both men and women (ONS, 1998, Tables 5.8 and 5.9). In other words, the rise in the proportion of female employees has been matched by a simultaneous fall in the number of male employees (Walby, 1997, Table 2.1). The proportion of women in the Netherlands who were employed was considerably less in 1996 (47 per cent), but the rise (from 29 per cent in 1975) was even more spectacular than in Britain (Keuzekamp and Oudhof, 2000).[1] In Germany, women's labour market participation rose from 46 per cent in 1970 to 61 per cent in 1998, while that of men fell from 88 to 80 per cent (Bundesanstalt für Arbeit, 1999).[2] In former East Germany, though, women's participation remains significantly higher, at 74 per cent in 1998. However, this compares to a pre-unification figure of 80 per cent, and has fallen relative to that of East German men during the 1990s, which bears out the point that female labour market participation rates may be converging between East and West. The most dramatic increases in all countries have been for women with children under five years of age; for example, the difference in activity rates between women with and without dependent children halved in Britain in the period from 1973 to 1996.

In Britain married women are as likely to be employed as non-married women and the contribution by men to family income fell from nearly 73 per cent in 1979–81 to 61 per cent in 1989–91 (Harkness, Machin, and Waldfogel, 1996). By 1996–7, women's contribution to a couple's joint lifetime earnings ranged from 41 per cent for a low-skilled woman without children to 49 per cent for a high-skilled woman, but dropped to 24

1 I am grateful to Dr Trudie Knijn, University of Utrecht, for this reference.
2 I am grateful to Professor Ute Gerhard, University of Frankfurt, for this reference.

per cent and 47 per cent respectively with the addition of two children, reflecting the large earnings gap between equally skilled men and women that hits low-skilled women particularly hard (Women's Unit, 1999). However, this figure varies widely across the European Union. In the Netherlands, men's average contribution to the household income amounted to 76 per cent in 1994. Some 10 per cent of women earned more than their husbands in 1994 and 7 per cent earned the same (Hooghiemstra, 1997). Arber and Ginn (1995) have shown that among dual-earner couples in the United Kingdom, only 6 per cent of employed women earn at least £40 per week more than their partners, and only 11 per cent of married women who work full-time have higher earnings than their husbands. In former West Germany in 1993 men contributed 73 per cent of income in households with children under 18, whereas men in former East Germany contributed 56 per cent. However, in the United States, where the real earnings of male manual workers have declined precipitously and where women are much more likely to work full-time, the percentage of marriages in which the husband provides 70 per cent or more of the couple's income declined from 78 to 46 per cent for whites between 1963 and 1992, and from 71 to 33 per cent for blacks (Smock and Gupta, 2000). Here, then, is more evidence of the emergence of a dual-earner model in which men and women make increasingly equal economic contributions.

The nature of women's participation in the labour market also varies considerably between countries. Table 13 shows the extent of women's part-time work, which varies enormously, but is highest in the countries of western and northern Europe and Australia. Men are still predominantly full-time workers everywhere, although Dutch men have higher rates of part-time employment than anywhere else. In North America a much greater proportion of women tend to work full-time, particularly in the United States. In addition, these women often work

TABLE 13
Female Part-time Employment as a Per Cent of Female Employment and Male
Part-time Employment as a Per Cent of Male Employment, 1983 and 1999

	1983 Male	1999 Male	1983 Female	1999 Female
Australia	9.2	14.3	35.5	41.4
Canada	8.7	10.3	28.1	28.0
Denmark	7.1	8.9	36.7	22.7
Finland	4.5	6.6	12.5	13.5
France	3.2	5.8	18.9	24.7
Germany	2.1	4.8	31.2	33.1
Ireland	3.2	7.9	17.4	31.9
Italy	3.7	5.3	16.5	23.2
Netherlands	5.6	11.9	44.7	55.4
Portugal	2.9*	5.0	12.2*	14.6
Spain	1.9[1]	2.9	12.1[1]	16.8
Sweden	4.9[1]	7.3	29.8[1]	22.3
UK	3.3	8.5	40.1	40.6
USA	9.1	8.1	22.9	19.0

*Data for 1986
[1]Data for 1987

Source: OECD, 2000, *Labour Force Statistics*, 1979–1999 (Paris: OECD Publications).

long hours. In 1998 in Canada, mothers aged 25–44 averaged 38.8 hours per week of paid work and work-related activities, an increase of 2 hours since 1992 (Statistics Canada, 1999). The meaning of part-time work also differs considerably between countries in terms of hours. In the United Kingdom, short part-time working is very common. Almost a quarter of women with children under the age of ten worked 15 or fewer hours per week in the late 1990s (Thair and Risdon, 1999), and 24 per cent of all female employees worked under 20 hours a week (Rubery, Smith, and Fagan, 1998). In the Netherlands 80 per cent of women worked part-time and 33 per cent worked less than 20 hours a week. In Germany women's participation is mainly part-time, and a quarter work fewer than 20 hours a week (the social insurance threshold). A further 18 per cent of German women work between 18 and 35 hours a week. In the Scandinavian countries, female part-time work among females is also common, but women usually work relatively long hours, often exercising their right to work part-time while they have young children. This part-time work attracts *pro rata* benefits and is not the 'precarious' employment that is so common in the United Kingdom.

These changes in labour market participation have not been accompanied by equality in respect of wages. In Britain the proportion of men's hourly wages earned by women who were working full-time rose from 63 per cent in 1970 to 80 per cent in 1995 (in Canada the figure was lower at 73 per cent). However, the hourly wage rate of part-time women workers compared to that of male workers narrowed only six percentage points over the same period and actually worsened relative to that of full-time women workers (Walby, 1997, Tables 2.4, 2.6). In the Netherlands the trend has been different: the gap between the hourly wages of men and women working full-time increased, while the wage gap between male and female part-time workers decreased.

Thus the precise nature of the erosion of the male-breadwinner model in respect of employment is complicated. There has been no simple move from a male earner to a dual-career model. Rather, in most Western countries some kind of dual-earner model has become the norm. Helen Jarvis's (1997) calculations as to the number of earners for a sample of married and cohabiting couples with dependent children, taken from the 1991 British Census, showed 55 per cent to have more than one earner, 36 per cent to have a single full-time earner, and 9 per cent to have no earners. While families supported solely by a male breadwinner are now undoubtedly in a minority – as a result mainly of women's increased contribution to the labour market, but also of the increased number of lone-mother households – the division of paid work in dual-earner couples takes a variety of forms. Dual *career* couples are relatively rare. The norm in the vast majority of countries has become a 'more-or-less one-and-a-half-earner household,' in other words the dual-earner models 1 and 2 in Figure 1. Model 3 is a more gender-equal model and has not been achieved in any country, but it is endorsed in the official policy of the Dutch government, with its 'combination scenario.' The Netherlands also has somewhat more part-time work for men (17 per cent of Dutch men work part-time, albeit that a majority of these are either young or over 55). Because of the high proportion of women working short part-time hours, together with the low hourly rates of pay for part-time women workers, in many dual-earner households the woman does not achieve even half the man's income. There are exceptions to the one-and-a-half earner model. In the United States and Finland women are much more likely to work full-time, and in Sweden women are as likely as men to be employed, but to work long part-time hours. It is in the United States and the Scandinavian countries that an adult-worker model has come closest to being realized, but, as Chapter 3 will point out, the *terms* on which this has been accomplished are very different indeed. While the United States has retained a firm public/private divide, making care work in the family a private responsibility, Scandinavian governments have sought actively to help to reconcile work and family responsibilities via the collective provision of cash and services.

Thus, the different patterns of paid employment in families and households are paralleled by different patterns of provision for care and, therefore, different gendered contributions to households in respect of unpaid work. We lack research on the precise nature of these patterns for different countries and what it is that has given rise to particular configurations. Using such national reports as there are, Figure 2 speculates on the nature of

Figure 2
Patterns of Male and Female Paid Work and Arrangements for Care

---

1. Male-Breadwinner Model

Male FT earner   Female FT carer

2. Dual-Breadwinner Model (I)

Male FT earner, female   Care supplied mainly by
short PT earner   female earner and kin

3. Dual-Breadwinner Model (II)

Male FT earner, female long PT   Care supplied mainly
earner   by kin, and state/voluntary/market
                                        sectors

4. Dual-Breadwinner Model (III)

Male PT earner, female PT   Care supplied by male and female
earner   earners

5. Dual Career

Male FT earner, female FT   Care supplied mainly by the
earner   market, and kin/state/voluntary
                                        sectors

6. Single Earner (Lone-Mother
   Family)

Female earner FT or PT, or FT   Care supplied either by the
mother reliant on state benefits   mother or by the mother, kin, and
                                        the state

---

care provision that accompanies different gendered patterns of paid and unpaid work. Hakim (1996, 2000) has argued strongly that the female labour market is divided into those who are committed to careers and those who see their paid work as secondary; in other words, the pattern of paid labour is a matter of choice. However, the availability of affordable and acceptable alternatives to unpaid care is also crucial. What is striking is the persistence of the gendered division of unpaid care work. There has been relatively little change in families in this respect. Indeed, it is only recently that women's much greater contribution to the unpaid work in households has received attention by academics. The early (1980s) literature on care emphasized the extent to which unpaid work was performed by women. Ann Oakley's (1974) pioneering research in the 1970s conceptualized housework as unpaid work; much research of the early 1980s differentiated care work from other forms of household labour (Finch and Groves, 1983). Falling fertility rates and the advent of birth control technology have meant that a much smaller proportion of women's lives are spent in caring for children. Titmuss (1958, p. 91) calculated that the average working-class British woman marrying in her teens or early twenties during the 1890s experienced ten pregnancies and spent fifteen years in pregnancy and nursing, compared with four years so spent by her counterpart in the years following the Second World War. With the decline in the years spent in childbearing, very sharply attenuated in some countries in the very recent past (see above, p. 20), and the improvement in women's health came concomitant possibilities for greater labour market attachment. On the other hand, aging populations mean that there are increasing numbers of elderly people who require informal care. As Table 14 shows, some of the southern European countries, where birth rates have fallen precipitously, will face particularly high numbers of retirees in the future.

Given the demographic trends in Western countries and in Japan, it is increasingly likely that 'women in the middle'

TABLE 14
Aging Population with Projections (per cent of total population)

	Age	1980	2000	2010	2030	2050
Australia	65+	9.6	12.1	13.4	20.0	22.6
	80+	1.7	2.8	3.4	5.2	7.6
Canada	65+	9.4	12.8	14.3	22.6	23.8
	80+	1.8	3.1	4.0	5.9	8.9
Denmark	65+	14.4	15.2	17.0	23.1	24.1
	80+	2.9	4.1	4.1	6.6	8.8
Finland	65+	12.0	14.9	17.0	25.3	25.6
	80+	1.8	3.4	4.5	7.7	9.7
France	65+	14.0	15.9	16.6	23.2	25.5
	80+	3.1	3.8	5.1	6.7	9.5
Germany	65+	15.6	16.4	19.8	26.1	28.4
	80+	2.8	3.6	4.8	6.8	11.3
Ireland	65+	10.7	11.3	12.2	17.9	23.3
	80+	1.8	2.6	3.0	4.6	6.7
Italy	65+	13.1	18.2	20.8	29.1	34.9
	80+	2.2	4.0	5.8	8.5	14.0
Netherlands	65+	11.5	13.8	15.8	25.6	28.1
	80+	2.3	3.3	4.1	6.9	11.3
Portugal	65+	10.5	15.7	17.1	22.9	31.2
	80+	1.4	3.1	4.3	5.9	9.6
Spain	65+	10.7	17.0	18.4	26.8	36.9
	80+	1.7	3.8	5.4	7.3	13.2
Sweden	65+	16.3	17.4	19.5	25.5	26.7
	80+	3.2	5.0	5.6	8.4	10.4
UK	65+	15.1	16.0	17.1	23.1	24.9
	80+	2.8	4.2	4.8	6.5	9.3
USA	65+	11.0	12.5	13.3	20.8	21.9
	80+	2.3	3.3	3.7	5.2	7.8

Source: ILO, 2000, *World Labour Report 2000* (Geneva: International Labour Organization).

(Brody, 1981) will find themselves caring for both children and elderly relatives at the same time. Since early northern European research on the number of carers, representative sample surveys have revealed that the largest category of carers are spouses and that as many as half of these are husbands (Arber and Ginn, 1991; Baines, Evans, and Neysmith, 1991). Nevertheless, women are the largest group of unpaid carers for elderly dependants, and there is substantial evidence to suggest that they do much more by way of intimate, personal care tasks. When there is a female carer on hand there is less likelihood of formal, public care being provided (Lewis, 1998). Time-use data for the United Kingdom during the 1990s have shown that the growth in married women's employment has slowly led to only a small reduction in the unequal gender division of unpaid work (Laurie and Gershuny, 2000).

Thus the social reality is that while a high proportion of adult women are in the workforce in most OECD countries, they are not fully individualized in the sense of being self-sufficient and they still take responsibility for a large proportion of the unpaid care work, supported to varying degrees by collective provision. The demographic case for increasing individualization seems somewhat stronger than that constructed on the basis of changing contributions to households. As the next chapter shows, the debate about these changes, in terms of their causes and their meanings, has been fierce.

2 〜〜

What Is
Family Change
About?
The Debate

THE LAST CHAPTER SHOWED THE COMPLEXITY of cross-national patterns in regard to demographic change and the nature of the contributions made by men and women to families. The debate about these changes has been highly charged, while relatively little attention has been paid to this cross-national complexity. Many dimensions of family change are seen as moral as well as social issues, which means that values have bulked large in the debate, certainly in the English-speaking countries. Continental Europeans have found it difficult to understand the passions that have been evoked by the increase in lone-mother families in English-speaking countries.

It is not surprising that rapid and profound changes in families have given rise to anxieties especially about the welfare of children. However, as Sara McLanahan and Karen Booth (1989) suggested, in the United States family change and lone motherhood in particular have generated a variety of fears: about the socialization of children, in terms of low levels of educational attainment and rising levels of criminality; about the role of women, particularly in terms of whether the mothers of young children should go out to work and the ramifications of greater female sexual autonomy; about the role of men, many of whom appear to be unwilling to shoulder financial responsibility for their children; and about racial tensions. All except the last of these concerns have also been expressed in the United Kingdom and Canada. Most strikingly, family change has been seen as bearing a large part of the responsibility for wide-scale social breakdown. Thus, the economist George Akerloff (1998) has argued that changes in marriage patterns are a more potent cause of social pathology in the form of criminal behaviour and drug abuse than unemployment or 'welfare dependency.' For Francis Fukuyama (1999), family change is part of the 'great disruption' in social norms and values that began in the 1960s and manifested itself in rising crime rates and a decline in trust, as well as in family breakdown. In Britain, Dennis and Erdos

(1992) sought to trace the rise of the 'obnoxious Englishman' to family breakdown.

Lone motherhood has thus been the focus of the most extreme anxieties and the most vituperative exchanges. By the end of the twentieth century one of the main focuses of the debate was the extent to which a whole range of changes in behaviour – in terms of women's work, marriage, divorce, extramarital birth, and cohabitation rates, as well as in lone motherhood – was the expression of a move towards greater individualism and hence selfishness. While individualism has been viewed as the motor of modern liberal market democracies, the family has historically been seen as a counterweight to the market, providing care and serving as the source of altruism and cooperation. Indeed, given that the traditional family has been assumed to be the bedrock of social, political, and economic thought, its apparent fragility at the end of the twentieth century aroused huge concern. Anxieties have turned on whether families will support and care for their members in the future, or whether family members were becoming more self-seeking, with the result that the traditional areas of 'family responsibility' for the care and maintenance of dependants is increasingly being passed to the state. The idea that family change has resulted in more dependence on the state – in 'welfare dependency,' to use the American expression – on the part of lone mothers, and in increased demands for state pensions for longer periods from higher numbers of elderly people, has attracted the attention of governments. Indeed, the widespread fall in birth rates, together with the rise in the numbers of old and very old people, has given rise to the fear of intergenerational conflict, particularly among academics in the United States and New Zealand. The conclusion from the work on 'generational accounting' (Kotlikoff, 1992) is that the current levels of social provision, particularly in respect of pensions, will be unaffordable and that more private provision is therefore inevitable (something I return to in Chapter 3).

In what follows, I look first at the debate over the rise of individualism, and then at the debate over three specific issues: absent fathers, the increasing economic independence of women, and the rise of cohabitation. Finally I return to the issue of obligation. It is this issue that preoccupies policymakers. They ask, will adult men and women support each other, will parents support children, and will the young support the old? But there are different ways of looking at obligation. While it cannot be denied that the traditional male-breadwinner family has been eroded, the fear that this has resulted in a vacuum which selfish individualism has filled is deduced from aggregate statistics rather than from what actually happens in families.

The Rise of Selfish Individualism?

The complicated nature of family change is open to huge differences in interpretation, especially given that there is no agreement on what the effects of the changes have been. The academic debate on family change has changed in tone since 1945. In the immediate postwar decades, the sociological accounts of the state of the family on both sides of the Atlantic stressed the fundamental stability of marriage (Fletcher, 1966; Young and Willmott, 1973; Goldthorpe et al., 1969; Bane, 1976). While sex was increasingly being separated from marriage, the premaritally pregnant tended to marry before the arrival of the child and divorce rates were still relatively low. The degree of family change therefore appeared slight. In Britain, Chester (1971) was one of a small minority who drew attention to the rising divorce rate of the 1960s and saw it as the product of something more than relaxed divorce laws, attributing the changes to a more permissive approach to personal behaviour. By the 1980s, this view had become much more prevalent. Writing in the *Journal of Family Issues* in 1987, Norval Glenn observed that leading

American writers were much less sanguine regarding the prospects of the American family in the mid-1980s than had been commentators a decade before.

The Findings from Empirical Research

On the whole, the findings from empirical research on family change have become more grim in the postwar period, although the data and methodology of these studies are always open to debate. During the 1950s and 1960s, British and American psychological, sociological, and medical research concluded that marital conflict was as bad for a child as divorce, and that divorce might actually be better for children than living with unhappy parents. But by the end of the 1970s, American research began to emphasize the bad effects of divorce on children's educational attainment, poverty levels, employment, and capacity to form stable relationships in their turn (Hetherington, Cox, and Cox, 1978; Wallerstein and Kelly, 1980), and it was not long before British empirical research followed suit (Richards and Dyson, 1982; Maclean and Wadsworth, 1988; Kiernan, 1992). Even though the evidence regarding the role of fathers in the lives of their children was mixed when Wallerstein and Kelly published their influential research in the United States (based on work with divorcing people who had sought counselling and were therefore by definition troubled), the opposing argument made no impact (Piper, 1993). Rather the policy debate seemed disposed to overturn the long-held emphasis on the importance of the mother/child dyad (reiterated as late as 1980 by Goldstein, Freud, and Solnit) in favour of 'bringing fathers back in.' A review of the literature on this topic by Rodgers and Pryor (1998) was cautious in its conclusions as to how far children's subsequent problems could be attributed to divorce per se, rather than to a range of factors that impinge on families before, during, and after separation. It is, after all, never possible to know the answer to the question, 'What if divorce had not happened?'

Studies of the effects of mothers' employment have been even more contradictory. A number of studies from the 1950s raised the spectre of juvenile crime among what were commonly referred to as 'latch-key children.' Yudkin and Holme (1963) concluded cautiously that it was imperative for mothers to stay at home with children under three years of age, but that beyond that, in 'favourable circumstances,' many children could do without their mother's constant presence. But findings on the issue of mothers going out to work have been very inconsistent. While the sudden rise in the divorce rate seemed to result in a series of studies questioning the desirability of the new trend, the gradual rise in women's employment has been subject to constant and contradictory comment. In 2000, researchers found some evidence that children's reading skills suffered if mothers worked while their children were under five years of age, but concluded that poverty, family history, and mothers' education were bigger influences (Joshi and Verropoulou, 2000). In 2001, British Household Panel Survey data comparing the differences in parents' employment patterns and outcomes between 516 pairs of siblings born in the 1970s showed that longer periods of full-time employment by the mothers of children under five tended to reduce a child's chances of obtaining a high-school qualification and to increase a child's risk of unemployment and psychological distress in early adulthood, but also tended to reduce the chances of daughters' giving birth before the age of 21 (Ermisch and Francesconi, 2001). The data and methodologies used in such research can always be questioned. In the case of the last of these studies, for example, it must be noted that the context for childrearing in the 1970s was very different, and the study did not take into account the quality of childcare.

Virtually all empirical studies on issues to do with family change are open to interpretation. This ambiguity allows those participating in the debate about the political and social significance of the changes to 'cherry-pick' the results that suit their arguments. For, in the end, the debate tends to be about what people feel is *driving* the changes; in other words, it is fuelled by beliefs about motivations as much as (the often conflicting) evidence on outcomes, and there is a strong tendency to believe that these motives are primarily selfish. It is this inclination that has made for more pessimism than optimism.

Ideas about Individualism

A number of recent demographic and historical studies have called attention to the growth in individualism (Van de Kaa, 1987; Macfarlane, 1986; Kiernan, Land, and Lewis, 1998). In such studies the various behavioural manifestations of family change, in terms of form, structure, and the contributions to family life made by men and women, are often taken as measures of individualism. Thus, for example, Van de Kaa's (1987) theory of a second demographic transition, beginning in the 1960s with the separation of sex and marriage and followed by the emergence of cohabitation, stressed the importance of the accompanying belief in the rights of the individual, especially in respect of personal and career fulfilment. The disputed territory is over the nature of individualism and its precise relationship with the observed changes in behaviour and family breakdown.

It has of course been widely recognized that the Western ideal of romantic love does not necessarily lead unproblematically to companionate marriage. Berger and Kellner (1964) portrayed marriage as a forging of a joint identity: couples wrote the marital script together. But there may be a fundamental tension between individual desire and the pursuit of individual happiness on the one hand, and loyalty to the marriage on the other. As Milton Regan (1999) has commented, society attaches a high value to both intimacy and individual autonomy. Individualism is at the heart of the idea of romantic love (Skolnick, 1991; Lystra, 1989) and may just as easily lead to adultery as towards monogamy. In her study of adultery, Lawson (1988, p. 26) wrote of the conflict between the 'myth of romantic marriage' and the 'myth of me,' which 'slips out from under' and propels the individual into an affair. As many writers – from de Rougemont in the 1940s to Luhman in the 1980s – have pointed out, marriage with love as its *raison d'être* is inherently unstable.

In fact it is the economics literature that has provided the firmest theoretical underpinnings for the idea of the importance of individual, rational choice and its application to the workings of the family. Neoclassical economists have suggested that as women are increasingly capable of supporting themselves, they have been less willing to put up with unsatisfactory marriages (Becker, Landes, and Michael, 1977). Gary Becker's (1981) work on a 'new home economics' argued that people marry when the utility expected from marriage is greater than it is if they remain single. Particularly if they want children, women will look for a good male breadwinner. Men will look for a good housekeeper and carer. Thus, men and women make complementary investments in marriage that result in higher joint gains. In fact there is nothing in Becker's model that is particular to marriage. Indeed, it may be just as applicable to cohabiting relationships. The laws of marriage and divorce, together with public policies, have historically assumed such a model to exist within marriage and have applied the model specifically to marital relationships. Becker's model assumes that gains are shared equally between husbands and wives (ignoring the possibility of a basic tension between an egalitarian, companionate ideal and the reality of inequalities in behaviour and rewards [Bernard, 1976; Skolnick, 1991]). In Becker's analysis, women's earning power disrupts the balance in the exchange of labour between husbands and wives and causes instability. Economic bargaining models (e.g., see Lundberg and Pollak, 1996) do not assume that resources are shared equally. Marital investment and exchange must offer both husbands and wives more than they obtain outside the marriage. According to these theories, a rise in women's employment, or an increase in their wages, will threaten the stability of marriage, because it will no longer offer women unequivocal gains. These kinds of analysis rely on the idea of individuals making rational choices to maximize their rewards and minimize their costs (Cheal, 1991).

The most pessimistic, polemical, and influential academic contributions to the debate have come from sociologists. In his statement on the family in 1987, Glenn suggested that if marriage were to be judged only by hedonistic standards it might become 'so insecure that no rational person will invest a great deal of time, energy, money and forgone opportunities to make a particular marriage satisfactory' (p. 351). Bellah et al.'s (1985) influential study of 'middle America' had already reached very similar conclusions: 'if love and marriage are seen primarily in terms of psychological gratification, they may fail to fulfil their older social function of providing people with stable, committed relationships that tie them into the larger society' (p. 85). Many American writers have been more circumspect in their judgments (e.g., Furstenburg and Cherlin, 1991; Coontz, 1991), but there is no doubt that the climate of opinion has shifted radically over the course of the last quarter of a century.

Bellah et al. (1985) opened their account of middle American life with the statement: 'We are concerned that this individualism may have grown cancerous' (p. vii). They identified two forms of individualism: first, the utilitarian, which amounted to the traditional American desire to 'get ahead' and to be self-reliant, and second, the expressive, which emphasized self-expression and the sharing of feelings rather than material acquisition. The perception of Bellah et al. was that the values of the public sphere – the 'coolly manipulative style' (p. 48) that is required to 'get-ahead' – were invading the private world of the family. This anxiety has a long history. The ideology of separate spheres – whereby the ruthless competition that was thought necessary for the successful operation of the market was balanced by the haven of the family, where women would care for the male worker and also for those too weak to engage in the public sphere – was central to turn-of-the-century classical liberalism (Lewis, 1984). In Bellah et al.'s view, the contractual structure of commercial and bureaucratic life threatened to become an ideology for personal life. Obligation and commitment would thereby be replaced by an ideology of full, open, and honest communication between self-actualizing individuals.

More polemically still, Popenoe, who first wrote critically of what he perceived as the collapse of the Swedish family (Popenoe, 1988) went on to argue that 'people have become less willing to invest time, money and energy in family life, turning instead to investment in themselves' (Popenoe, 1993, p. 528). The inference in this statement is that growing individualism is based on selfishness. This view was taken up in the British Parliamentary debates over the 1996 Family Law Act, during the course of which many members of Parliament sought to make the legislation a vehicle for saving marriage. In the House of Lords, Baroness Young said that 'for one party simply to decide to go off with another person ... reflects the growing *self-first disease* which is debasing our society' (Hansard, Lords, 29/2/96, c. 1638, italics added). Policy makers during the 1990s have clearly expressed their fear of increasing individualism, which they have automatically assumed to be based on selfishness and considered the natural antithesis of interdependence (Smart and Neale, 1997).

Bellah et al. (1985) suggested that the pursuit of personal growth begins with the self rather than an external set of obligations and that love between 'therapeutically self-actualized persons' is incompatible with self-sacrifice. The strong belief in personal freedom and the rights of the rational, individual actor to make choices unfettered by regulation that characterized both Thatcherism and Reaganism in the 1980s also played a major part in this process of separating feeling from its social constraints. Reflecting on the politics of Thatcherism, Marilyn Strathern (1992) identified the emergence of a 'hyper-individualism,' where morality, like everything else, is a matter of individual choice and preference. Morality may come from within, 'but the interior has itself no structure' (p. 159). As Sandel (1982) had already suggested, a person without constitutive attachments is a person wholly without character. Strathern questioned the effect of the fetishization of individual choice, arguing that individuality becomes fragmented in the face of such a 'consumerist' ideology (see also Gergen, 1991). The difficulty of exercising choice in a moral and social vacuum has become an increasingly dominant theme in the literature.

This compelling picture of a world in which there is no vision of the common good and in which rampant individualism is destroying the very foundations – the family and the community – on which the market and modern liberal democracies depend has been widely echoed. While polemicists railed against what they perceived as selfish behaviour, academics began to try and find ways to talk about the importance of 'social glue.' Thus Coleman (1988) used the concept of social capital, that is, the informal values and norms that enable a group of people to work together, as a way of challenging the rational individual action paradigm. In the context of the family, social capital consists of the relationship between the parents and the children, which gives the child access to the parents' resources, intellectual, material, and emotional. Social capital as a set of informal values and norms fosters cooperation and trust (Coleman, 1988; Fukuyama, 1999). Trust and cooperation are learned in the private sphere of the family (and in civil society [Putnam, 1993]) and carried into the public sphere of politics and the market. Feminists have long insisted upon the importance of connection and the relational self to women's moral sense (Gilligan, 1982; Held, 1993; Griffiths, 1995). The recent literature on social capital represents a wider appreciation of the fact that no one is an 'unencumbered self' (Sandel, 1996), and that interdependence, and hence the obligations people have towards one another, are important.

Family change is, then, particularly susceptible to being interpreted in terms of selfish individualism, whether the focus be the behaviour of men, women, or the changing nature of intimate relationships themselves. For example, take the shift from marriage to cohabitation. Are people just more willing to walk out of relationships, even where there are children, on grounds that earlier generations might have judged to be little more than a whim? Are people more concerned with self-fulfilment than with caring for the needs of others?

Not all commentators are prepared to answer a simple yes, especially those who focus more on changes in the nature of intimate relationships and on their *meanings* (e.g., Giddens, 1992; Cancian, 1987). These writers, rather than inferring motivation from aggregate statistics, tend to see a more complicated set of changes in values and obligations than those who, like Popenoe (1993), focus on the behavioural outcomes of family change and then read off motivation from them. Giddens' (1992) notion of 'pure relationship' suggested that in the late twentieth-century relationships were 'entered into for [their] own sake, for what can be derived by each person from a sustained association with another; and which is continued only in so far as it is thought by both parties to deliver enough satisfactions for each individual to stay within it' (p. 35). Unlike Bellah et al., Giddens does not consider such relationships to be inherently selfish; rather, he believes that they have served to democratize the family. Nevertheless, relationships are 'contingent' and if a particular relationship does not provide one of the partners with what they seek, then he or she will move on.

The data presented in the last chapter indicate that on the

work and family front we are seeing more evidence of individualization. Beck Gernsheim (1999, p. 54) has described the effects
of individualization on the family in terms of 'a community of
need' becoming 'an elective relationship.' Elias (1991) expressed
a similar idea: 'The greater impermanence of we-relationships,
which at earlier stages often had the lifelong inescapable character of an external constraint, puts all the more emphasis on the I,
one's own person, as the only permanent factor, the only person
with whom one must live one's whole life' (p. 204). If the family
used to be more of a community of need, held together by the
obligations of solidarity, then women's increased labour market
participation, together with family instability, has resulted in
new divisions between biography and family. In other words,
dual breadwinning, along with the unpredictable ordering of
intimate relationships and childbearing, poses problems for the
maintenance and support of dependent family members. Burns
and Scott (1994) have made a similar point in their discussion of
the ways in which male and female roles in the family have
become 'decomplementary.' Again, these explanatory frame-
works do not seek to deny the importance of the changes that
have taken place, but incorporate the parts played by structural
change and individual choice.

The idea that there has been a growth in individualism in personal relationships bears some relation to the long-held notion
that marriage has moved from being an institution to a relationship (Lewis, Clark, and Morgan, 1992). Many believe that those
involved in intimate relationships have become less conscious
of their 'public,' social dimensions – in terms of the duties owed
to one another, to their children, and even to the wider kin
group – and have increasingly limited their attention to the
quality of the relationship itself and the calculus of benefits and
dis-welfares to themselves as individuals. Furstenberg and
Cherlin (1991) have suggested that emotional exchange has
become primary in relationships. However, de Singly (1996) has

seen this as more the case for men than for women, given the unequal gendered division of paid and unpaid work. Théry (1994) has suggested that marriage has become a private choice and that marriage as an institution has become disengaged from wider social structures. If true, this would mean that marriage has come more closely to resemble cohabitation. Nevertheless, while cohabitation rates have risen dramatically, marriage is far from dead. In the majority of cases, cohabitation is still followed by marriage, signifying that people do recognize the distinction. Indeed, Gillis (1997) has turned the argument on its head by suggesting that all intimate relationships now resemble conjugal ones; 'the perfect couple,' loving and committed, has become the standard for premarital and cohabiting relationships.

The issue of individualism in intimate relationships has been analysed in very different ways. Some researchers have focused on a particular kind of behaviour associated with family change, in particular the increased failure of men to support their families and the increased economic independence of women. Others focus more on the meaning of relationships themselves and emphasize structural and cultural variables. There is no consensus in either group of writings on the question of growing selfishness.

Key Issues in the Debate

Absent Fathers: Men's Failure to Pay Support

The role of fathers in traditional families was conceptualized in terms of financial provision, and it was marriage that activated the male-breadwinner model for policy-making purposes. As lone mothers became much more numerous in the late twentieth century, and the role of father could no longer be automatically linked to that of husband, the issue of fathers' responsibilities began to be raised explicitly. Marriage law could no longer be relied on to secure parental responsibility.

The focus on fathers since the end of the 1980s was new in relation to the rest of the postwar period, but in fact reflected much older concerns familiar to commentators at the beginning of the century. In 1906, Helen Bosanquet, referred to earlier in this book, emphasized the connection between the stable family and the importance of maintaining work incentives for men. She was not alone in suspecting working-class fathers especially of an unwillingness to shoulder their economic responsibilities. Other Edwardian investigators firmly believed that married women's employment merely provided their husbands with the opportunity to be idle. The economist F.Y. Edgeworth (1922) endorsed a statement a social worker made in 1908 recommending that 'if the husband got out of work, the only thing the wife should do is sit down and cry, because if she did anything else he would remain out of work' (p. 453). Only the advent of mass unemployment in the interwar years modified this view somewhat. The value of family life as a means of making men 'useful' members of society was again emphasized in the late twentieth century.

In the wake of the Second World War, there was much greater sympathy with the father than previously. Several commentators were uneasy about the father's position, believing that the changes in the legal status of women – for example, the move towards a more equitable divorce law, guardianship rights over children, and suffrage – posed a threat to the father's authority (e.g., Spence, 1946). Bertrand Russell, who took a consistently radical line throughout the early part of the century in demanding marriage and divorce law reform, also deplored the decline in the role of the father. He felt that the paternalist state and the caring professions removed the father's *raison d'être* by providing his children with free school meals and medical attention and usurped his authority via the school and the juvenile court (Russell, 1929).

After 1945, the cooperation of fathers tended to be assumed. The work habits of working-class men, who had proved themselves in battle, were no longer regarded with such suspicion, and experts focused their attention firmly on mother and child, whether in terms of the studies of maternal deprivation (Riley, 1983) or maternal 'adequacy.' The leading child psychologist, D.W. Winnicott (1957), said that the father was needed to help the mother feel well in body and happy in mind and to give her moral support, especially in matters of child discipline. The father's role was of marginal importance when it came to the care of his children. In the increasingly dominant 'expert' psychoanalytical social-work literature of the immediate postwar years unmarried fathers were constructed much as unmarried mothers were: as abnormal and as victims. The unmarried mother was described in pathological terms and the unmarried father was the 'counterpart of the neurotic personality of the unmarried mother' (L. Young, 1954).

Fathers were largely absent from debates over policy making and academic discourse until the late 1980s, when the political debate was dominated by those who stressed the irresponsibility and selfishness of men as well as of women. Michael Howard, then British Home Secretary, said in a speech to the Conservative Political Centre in 1993: 'If the state will house and pay for their children the duty on [young men] to get involved may seem removed from their shoulders ... And since the State is educating, housing and feeding their children the nature of parental responsibility may seem less immediate' (Howard, 1993). This reaction was very similar to Gilder's (1981) claim that in the United States the father 'has been cuckolded by the compassionate state,' as well as to Helen Bosanquet's concerns expressed in 1906. Howard went on to argue that the father's duty to support his family was important in terms of the role model it provided for children, and also of fairness to the taxpayer: 'When a family breaks up, the husband's standard of living often rises whereas that of his wife and children falls, even below the poverty line. Taxpayers may then be left to support the first family, while the husband sets about forming another. This is wrong. A father who can afford to support only one family ought to have only one' (*The Economist*, leader, 9 September 1995). Such views stood in stark contrast to the attitudes expressed some twenty years earlier in the *Report of the Royal Commission on One-Parent Families in the UK* (Cmd. 5629, 1974). The report recognized the difficulty in a liberal democratic society of determining who had the right to procreate, and of enforcing measures to stop further reproduction on the part of men, recommended that the state was bound to support the mothers and children left behind.

The prime concern of commentators about men's obligation to support was often allied with a more general concern about an increase in male irresponsibility. All argued that the successful socialization of children requires the active involvement of two parents. When Dennis and Erdos (1992) sought to trace the rise of the 'obnoxious Englishman' to family breakdown, their chief concern was the effect of lone motherhood on the behaviour patterns of young men. They blamed lone motherhood for, at best, irresponsible and, at worse, criminal behaviour in the next male generation. In fact such convictions about the link between absent fathers and rising crime rates have not been tested for any large-scale British sample. Halsey (1993) believed that 'the traditional family is the tested arrangement for safeguarding the welfare of children and that only a post-Christian country could believe otherwise.' In his view, the greed and individualism engendered during the Thatcher years were largely responsible for the disintegration of the traditional family. Others, while not blaming individualism, argued for more incentives, for example in the form of the married man's tax allowance, to the formation of traditional two-parent, male-breadwinner families (see, e.g., Morgan, 1995).

The assumption behind much of this literature is that men are instinctively uncivilized and that family responsibility is the only thing that ties them into communal living. Dench (1994) argued strongly that family responsibilities are an indispensable civilizing influence on men:

> If women go too far in pressing for symmetry, and in trying to change the rules of the game, men will simply decide not to play ... If women now choose to ... withdraw the notion that men's family role is important, then they are throwing away their best trick. Feminism, in dismantling patriarchy, is simply reviving the underlying greater natural freedom of men ... Many women are now setting great store by the coming of New Man ... the current attack on patriarchal conventions is surely promoting almost the exact opposite, namely a plague of feckless yobs, who leave all the real work to women and gravitate towards the margins of society where males naturally hang around unless culture gives them a reason to do otherwise. The family may be a myth, but it is a myth that works to make men tolerably useful. (pp. 16–17)

In this interpretation, as much blame is attributed to women as to men themselves for undermining the traditional male role of breadwinner. The influential British journalist Melanie Phillips (1997) also concluded that it is the erosion of the male role that has created 'yobbish men.'

This view has much in common with some feminist analysis (e.g., Ehrenreich, 1983) in so far as it diagnoses the problem in terms of male flight. In her commentary Stacey (1990) cited a sample of young working-class men in California who were not sure whether to regard one of their number who became a breadwinner as a hero or a chump. However, in this regard the analysis of feminists differs profoundly from that of academics and commentators who identify the problem in terms of the erosion of the male role and who seek to turn the clock back to recapture something approaching the 1950s family, with clearly segregated roles between men and women. In any case, as American sociologists and demographers have pointed out, the fall in male manual workers' earnings during the 1980s and 1990s has made it impossible for many to act as breadwinners (W.J. Wilson, 1987; Oppenheimer, 1994; Luker, 1996). As the last chapter showed, the evidence from many countries indicates that men's contribution to the family economy has diminished. In other words, structural change may be as or more important a factor in behaviour than male irresponsibility or the female pursuit of self-fulfilment.

The identification of male behaviour as problematic in the 1990s, and at the beginning of the twentieth century, was based on the fear that, given the opportunity, men would pursue their own selfish interests and ignore the welfare of their families. Cohen (1987) used Becker's ideas about the gains expected from marriage by women and men (see above, p. 53) to draw attention to the possibilities for opportunistic behaviour on the part of men. Cohen pointed out that investments in marriage are front-loaded for women because of childbearing. The relative decline in the value of women on the marriage market exposes them to the risk of the expropriation of the greater investment they make early on in marriage – their 'quasi-rents' – by their husbands. In Cohen's analysis, it was the introduction of no-fault divorce that permitted men to follow their 'natural' inclinations and behave opportunistically. Posner (1992) has also argued that if divorce law does not insist on proper compensation for the woman's greater and earlier investment it will serve to destabilize marriage.

Thus, the analysis of male behaviour has, like the literature from the early part of this century, tended to assume that men are 'naturally' inclined to individualistic behaviour and that changes in the law have facilitated such behaviour. The main divergence in views lies between those who are ready to blame men for acting selfishly, and those who are more likely to invoke structural change or to blame women for pushing men into such behaviour.

Women's Increasing Economic Independence

Women have also been seen as pursuing a more individualist course, which is sometimes construed as a search for self-fulfilment at the expense of other family members, and which is measured by women's increasing economic independence either by wage-earning or dependence on state benefits rather than on their husbands. Changes in women's labour market participation have been dramatic. This issue has a much longer history in the postwar period than the issue of male irresponsibility, and has been much more fully explored in a range of academic disciplines. As Oppenheimer (1994) has pointed out, the belief that women's increased economic independence has an effect on their marital behaviour is widespread, possibly because people with very different politics can buy into it. Both Gilder (1987) in the United States and Dench (1994) in Britain see the increase in adult women's labour force participation and attachment as something that has stripped men of their traditional breadwinning role within the family, and they blame women for pursuing self-fulfilment in the form of a career at the expense of their families. But feminists are as likely to endorse a theory that stresses the importance of women's economic independence as are right-wing polemicists, while of course stressing women's right and/or need to work.

Neoclassical economists have suggested that as women's capacity to support themselves has increased they have been less willing to put up with unsatisfactory marriages (Becker, Landes, and Michael, 1977). The fact that the majority of petitioners for divorce are female is taken as evidence of the growth in women's individualistic behaviour. However, there are many other explanations for the numbers of female petitioners. Men tend to react to breakdown with violence or by walking out of the relationship, leaving women to seek divorce (Phillips, 1988). As the economically weaker partner, the woman usually needs to try to get the financial arrangements settled (Maclean, 1991). As the last chapter demonstrated, women have continued to be economically dependent because of short-time working and low pay (see also Sorenson and McLanahan, 1987).

It is unlikely that greater financial independence is in and of itself the primary impetus to women seeking divorce. Cherlin (1981) argued that the increase in women's employment did not *cause* the increase in divorce but had made it more feasible. Beck and Beck Gernsheim (1995), who focus their attention more on meanings than behaviour, have argued that whereas mothers wholly dependent on men for economic support used to abandon their hopes, women who now have some means of supporting themselves have the possibility of choosing to abandon the marriage. De Singly (1996) suggests again that it is not paid employment *per se* that is responsible for women's greater readiness to consider divorce, but rather the awareness it creates of tensions within the marriage.

In the case of the young, unmarried mother, who, in the socially polarized English-speaking countries is likely to have little education and few skills, the postponement of childbirth by two or three years is unlikely to radically affect her prospects, especially given the fact that the unmarried father is probably a low earner or unemployed (Phoenix, 1991). The baby provides a passport to adult status, although there is little evidence to support the fiercely political argument advanced by conservative commentators in the United States during the 1980s (Murray, 1984) that young unmarried mothers get pregnant in order to claim welfare benefits and thus to receive a measure of economic independence courtesy of the state rather than the labour market (Ellwood and Bane, 1985). The increase in female employment and the availability of state benefits may be held to facilitate rather than cause family breakdown, and thus the search for explanations of family change extends beyond the economic.

It is unlikely that women abide solely by the dictates of economic rationality in making decisions about marriage, divorce, and motherhood. Alternative value systems that give priority to emotional satisfaction and care may be as important elements in the explanation of their behaviour in intimate relationships. Bellah et al. (1985) interpreted the desire for emotional satisfaction in terms of self-interest, but it may be the lack of interdependence in the sense of emotional support that triggers breakdown rather than the selfish pursuit of personal growth. It may also be that (possibly selfish) individualism is the outcome rather than the determinant of changes in economic and social behaviour. The basic premise of Burns and Scott's (1994) idea of 'decomplementarity' is that men and women have become more independent of each other. Oppenheimer (1994) has suggested something similar, positing a new collaborative model of marriage, which she argues has replaced the old specialization of men as breadwinners and women as housewives and carers. In this new form, marriage is based on the ability of each partner to make a contribution, unique or similar, and to pull his or her weight in the relationship. In this view, the change in behaviour is rational and has the benefits of increased freedom and independence, as well as the potential problems resulting from the greater propensity of a dissatisfied partner to exit from the relationship.

Recent academic work has shown more appreciation of the importance of cultural variables. Lesthaeghe and Surkym (1988) have argued that culture is an integral rather than an exogenous variable, as the neoclassical economists would have it. For example, many unhappily married women stayed married in the past because of the powerful stigma of divorce. Thus Bane and Jargowsky (1988, p. 246) concluded at the end of their empirical work, which considered only economic variables and found them wanting, that 'our hunch is that the real force behind family change has been a profound change in people's attitudes about marriage and children.' Attitudes, values, and beliefs are not easy to deal with. Sociologists disagree, for example, as to whether increased female employment is linked to more egalitarian gender-role attitudes (Haller and Hollinger, 1994; Alvin, Braun, and Scott, 1992). Nevertheless, as Oppenheim Mason and Jensen (1995) have pointed out, the microtheory of the neoclassicist economists does not recognize or allow for collectively generated or agreed-upon norms and sanctions. Yet the meaning that is attached by the majority to marriage (and to cohabitation) and to the contributions that men and women bring to it may well have changed (Manting, 1996). If indeed it has become important to maximize income, then high-earning women may be more likely to marry and less likely to divorce, the opposite of Becker's predictions. In addition, women's increased labour market participation may lead them to prioritize sexual satisfaction and emotional companionship over their husbands' capacity to provide, areas in which more men may fall short. This example shows the importance of considering how the relationship between social, economic, and legal changes and changing family structure are mediated by changes in ideas about marriage and family life.

The Rise of Cohabitation

The fear that cohabitation may be increasing at the expense of marriage has been heightened by concern that cohabitation appears to be relatively impermanent and a less 'committed' form of relationship, with higher rates of dissolution. Indeed, a Canadian study that attempted to operationalize Giddens' concept of the 'pure relationship,' in which the partners are committed only for as long as they feel that they personally benefit, concluded that cohabitants came closest to matching the criteria developed (Hall, 1996). It is tempting to conclude that the process of 'individualization,' which according to Beck and Beck Gernsheim (1995) pulls men and women apart, but at the same time makes a close relationship attractive, would favour cohabitation over marriage.

Nevertheless, there are many different forms of cohabitation and the reasons for each may be very different (McRae, 1997). In addition, interpretations of the research findings vary widely. Premarital cohabitation has long been justified as a form of trial marriage. Gillis (1986) has suggested that it resembles older patterns of betrothal. Certainly the average duration of premarital cohabitation closely mirrors the traditional period of engagement. Cohabitants were asked by the British Household Panel Survey in 1998 what they expected the outcome of their relationship to be, and 70 per cent answered 'marriage,' although in fact only 60 per cent went on to marry. However, American research has indicated that the effect of premarital cohabitation on marriage may actually be negative (Thomson and Colella, 1992). Indeed Cherlin (1992), who is considerably less pessimistic regarding family change than many of his US contemporaries, has argued that cohabitation is a relationship that the parties believe should be ended if it fails to provide satisfaction, and that people take these attitudes into marriage: 'Cohabitation comes with the ethic that a relationship should be ended if either partner is dissatisfied; this after all is part of the reason why people live together rather than marrying. Consequently the spread of cohabitation involves the spread of an individualistic outlook on intimate relations' (pp. 15–16). Rindfuss and VandenHeuvel (1990) found that among their young cohabitants, cohabitation was seen as a way of securing intimacy without making any long-term commitment. The findings of Schoen (1992) and Clarkberg, Stolzenberg, and Waite et al. (1995) were similar, and stressed the liberal values of cohabitants and the way in which these were indicators of preferences for a type of relationship that was essentially different from marriage.

Some cohabitants may avoid entering a legally constructed relationship in order to make it easier to move on if it does not meet their expectations. Some may make a principled decision about cohabitation being more suited to a relationship in which both contribute equally. The idea of the 'pure relationship' is premised upon a degree of equality between the partners and assumes a large measure of material well-being. Smart and Stevens (2000) have referred to those making a principled decision about cohabitation as 'reflexive.' However, others may be responding to difficult circumstances. Living together is popular among both students and the young unemployed. Cohabitants in the United Kingdom who do not marry are more likely to have lower levels of education, to have no religious affiliation, and to have experienced the divorce or separation of their parents (Kiernan, 1999). McRae (1993) investigated 228 mothers who had cohabited either before or in place of marriage and 100 never-cohabiting married mothers. She concluded that cohabitation represented a 'rational response' to low male wages and economic insecurity (see also Ermisch and Francesconi, 1998). Marriage is 'practised most often by those with something to transact' (McRae, 1993, p. 106). In this analysis, it is material circumstances rather than values that are most important in explaining this form of cohabitation, which is why Smart and Stevens (2000) have called this low-income group the 'rational risk takers.' In fact, the majority of UK cohabitants with children are disproportionately ill-educated, young, and poor.

Marriage became virtually universal in the immediate postwar decades and has seemingly become much less popular in the closing years of the century. In the view of Newcomb (1981), cohabitation meets the desire for individualism and intimacy, but it may just as plausibly be argued that it meets the needs of late twentieth-century young people who became sexually active earlier and remain economically dependent longer (de Singly, 1996), young people who are sexually active with no property and few skills, or of women who experience conflict between a desire for autonomy and the sanctions of marriage (Adams, 1998).

To some extent, all of these explanations see the emergence of cohabitation as a rational solution to complicated changes in beliefs, behaviour, and circumstances. It is difficult to make simple links between patterns of less marriage, more cohabitation, and more individualism. Cohabitation is now both alternative and sequential to marriage; many people will experience both at different points in the life course. Haskey's (1995, 1999) analysis shows that patterns of marriage, divorce, singlehood, and cohabitation are becoming increasingly complicated within the life course of individuals. Periods of cohabitation may precede marriage and follow divorce. Whereas in the nineteenth century marriage rates were a reasonable proxy for the employment rate, this was no longer so in the late twentieth century. Better wages together with a national minimum level of welfare secured by the state have ensured that people can adopt the kind of postmaterialist values identified by Inglehart (1997). Following the ideas of Beck and Beck Gernsheim, Kuijsten (1996) concluded that there is 'convergence towards diversity' as individuals construct new biographical models involving serial cohabitations, marriages, and divorces. It is not possible to characterize cohabitation as a form in keeping with a shift towards selfish individualism. However, marriage has certainly become much less of a common experience (Nock, 1995).

The Self and the Other: The Issue of Obligations

Cancian's (1987) study of love in America stressed the extent to which individualism was not necessarily antithetical to feelings of responsibility for the welfare of others. Many of the couples in her sample sought interdependence in the context of greater individualization. Pahl (1996) has emphasized the importance of distinguishing between individualism and individuality. Interdependent people can value personal growth, individuality, equality, and a morality that comes from within rather than one that is imposed from without and yet still feel committed to one another. However, because such commitment is not socially prescribed, it is seen as individualistic. Lesthaeghe (1995) has put forward the concept of 'individual autonomy,' which in his view has nothing to do with egocentric behaviour. It means only that the individual no longer takes externally supplied norms and morality for granted, and exercises instead his or her freedom of choice. Beck and Beck Gernsheim (1995) argue that it is no longer possible to say what family, marriage, parenthood, sexuality, and love mean. All vary in substance and interpretation, from individual to individual and from relationship to relationship. The collective norm seems to be that there is no norm.

The traditional male-breadwinner model family may never have characterized the social reality for large numbers of people, but it worked powerfully at the level of prescription. It was the 'ought' in terms of relationships between men and women and was underpinned by social policies, which assumed female dependence on a male wage, and by family law, which made the same assumptions about the marriage contract in terms of stability and the nature of the contribution of men and women in families, and implemented them through fault-based divorce (Weitzman, 1985). Men as husbands (and fathers) were cast as providers and women as wives (and mothers) as carers. Because of the stability of both marriage and of expectations concerning male and female responsibilities within the family, it was possible for family law and public policy to treat husbands/fathers and wives/mothers as unitary categories. This model has been substantially eroded both at the level of behaviour (as we saw in Chapter 1), but also at the level of normative prescription. This is why the debate over family change has been so fierce. The fear is that a vacuum has been created and that as a result people are doing as they please. However, Bauman (1993, 1995) has argued that deregulation and the removal of rules has not meant that people have abandoned the responsibility for making ethical choices. Karst (1980) found that intimate relationships generate moral obligations even when law does not enforce them. Divorce, for example, has become easier to obtain than in the past, but this does not necessarily mean that moral debate and responsibility have been eliminated.

Academics from a variety of disciplines and political positions have shown that people do employ 'moral sense' (J.Q. Wilson, 1993) and take their obligations to others seriously. Finch and Mason (1993) found in their empirical study of family obligations between the generations that people continually negotiate their commitments to one another over time and that their commitments extend beyond material considerations. Much more complicated ideas involving desert and reputation were involved. Finch and Mason stressed that while Becker was right in perceiving the essence of commitment to reside in the fact that it becomes at some point too expensive to withdraw, the nature of the expense is not necessarily material. Indeed, the gloomy statistics from those preoccupied with the cost of the generational contract ignore the voluntary transfers of wealth, and more important still, the transfers in the form of unpaid care work that go on between the generations. One of the most suggestive trends in recent empirical work has been the idea that, while at the demographic level, families and family building are becoming ever more diverse, there is convergence in terms of the negotiated nature of commitment and responsibility (Weeks, Donovan, and Heaphy, 1999).

Fears about increasing individualism in intimate relationships are grounded in the idea that it is incompatible with commitment. Men are assumed to be naturally inclined to selfish and irresponsible behaviour if not tied into families, and evidence of women's greater labour market participation is taken as evidence of more egocentric behaviour on their part. Those who are pessimistic about the nature of late twentieth-century family life have linked behavioural change to family breakdown and have tended to see increased individualism as the motive behind behavioural change. But, while greater female employment may well facilitate family change, it is unlikely to cause it. Burns and Scott (1994) and Oppenheimer (1994) have stressed the extent to which behavioural change is a rational adaptation to changed circumstances. Change is as likely to produce individualism as individualism is likely to be the cause of change.

Those who have paid more attention to the changing nature of intimate relationships themselves have offered a more nuanced picture of individualism and have on the whole been less ready to interpret it either negatively or pessimistically. A greater emphasis on individual autonomy, both economic and moral, may result in different priorities being attached to the qualities sought from a marriage partner or a cohabitant. This trend is not necessarily accompanied by a decline in commitment. It is unlikely that there is any simple relationship between individualism and changes in marital behaviour of the kind proposed by authors such as Popenoe. However, as Giddens (1992) and Beck and Beck Gernsheim (1995) have stressed, the way in which social and economic change is expressed in changing values and norms is important. This is also the case in respect of legal change. Social policy, particularly in the form of social security law, has similarly been shown to facilitate rather than cause family change. But it may nevertheless serve to legitimize certain kinds of behaviour. In addition, family law and social policies have to respond to family change, for example, to the increasing separation between the status of husband and father, and wife and mother.

A large part of the debate has been about what legislation can and should do. As the next chapter will show, the positions again tend to be polarized. Those who fear that the reasons for family change are the result of selfish behaviour are inclined to want to put the clock back, but this is difficult, not least because the commentators who are most concerned about family change also tend to be the ones most committed to family privacy. On the other hand, those who worry most about the cost of family change to the state in the form of benefits and pensions are likely to promote some kind of change, particularly increased female employment, in an effort to ensure that individuals become more self-provisioning. There are various options to consider in responding to family change, but we may have to look beyond the English-speaking world for models.

3

What Can Be
Done about
Family Change?
Issues for
Family Law and
Public Policy

THE FAMILY OBLIGATIONS THAT INTEREST POLICY MAKERS revolve mainly around the maintenance and care of children by parents, of elderly parents by children, and, to a lesser extent, between adult partners, especially if one is caring for a child. Given the demographic trends, policy makers may also be increasingly interested in the extent to which adults feel obliged to care for each other in old age (spouses are the most numerous group of informal carers), which again begs the question of the degree of commitment in personal relationships among today's working-age population. Most attention has focused on parental obligations, but given the fact that it is usually women who care for children, financial support for mothers is also an issue when relationships break down.

The traditional male-breadwinner model family was presumed to provide a stable source of support – in terms of both cash and care – for its members. Indeed, the family has always been the most important source of welfare provision, more so than the state or the voluntary sector. Policy makers have therefore been anxious about the implications of the erosion of the traditional family. What should be the response of both private family law and public policy to the many issues raised by family change? Do the changes in family structure, together with the greater labour market participation on the part of women, make it inevitable – and indeed desirable – that legislators treat men and women on an equal and individual basis?

Behind these issues lies the question of the obligations of men and women to each other and to their children and what government can or should do to uphold these obligations. The instinct of many politicians is to promote the *status quo ante*, but if that is not acceptable to large segments of the population and therefore not politically feasible, should government be thinking about new ways of regulating the family, perhaps by getting people to sort out their own problems, for example, via the use of contracts, and/or of ways of working with the process of change rather than seeking to put the clock back? In taking any action, governments must deal with the issue of family privacy. Conservative support for the traditional family is strong, but it also favours a firm division between the public and private spheres. In terms of family law, the trend since the 1960s and 1970s has been towards greater 'private ordering,' which allows the individuals effectively to make their own decisions, particularly in respect of divorce. However, the issues raised in regard to children and parenthood have complicated the picture. As Chapter 1 showed, men and women are not equally individualized, with women still doing the bulk of unpaid care work, and this inequality poses problems for the kind of 'clean-break' agreements that were favoured by divorce courts during the 1980s.

In respect of public policy, governments in the English-speaking world have shown signs in the 1990s of accepting the trend towards individualization signalled by both new family structures and women's employment, and of beginning to treat all adults as 'citizen workers.' Fears about the impact of globalization and the need for greater competitiveness and more flexible employment have coalesced with concerns about the costs of aging populations to promote an 'adult worker' rather than a 'male breadwinner' model family. But, again, the unequal, gendered division of labour, and hence of resources, poses problems for this strategy, which does not, for example, address the problem of poverty experienced by lone mothers and their children. It also has major implications for the unpaid care of the young and old traditionally carried out in the family.

Patterns of Obligation in Traditional Marriage

Public policies have historically assumed a division of responsibility between the obligation to pay support, assigned to the male-breadwinner husband, and the unpaid work of housework and caring, assigned to wives (Land, 1980; Lewis, 1992).

Other dimensions of the marriage contract play a part in underpinning this pattern of obligation. Pateman (1988) has insisted that marriage is above all a heterosexual contract, which explains why gay people have been excluded from it. Marriage legitimizes access to sex for men and it is the sacramental dimension of marriage that hides the essential subordination of women. In both public and private law, a firm link has been established between sex and support for both cohabiting and marital relationships. If a woman cohabits, her partner is assumed to be supporting her, and if she is in receipt of any state benefits, she is liable to lose them. During the 1970s, there was considerable protest from feminists about government officials looking for evidence of a sexual relationship between unmarried partners in order to cut off welfare benefits, as a way of enforcing what was known in Canada as the 'man-in-the-house' rule. While assumptions regarding gender roles may be stronger for the married, they have not been entirely absent for cohabitants. However, marriage has historically attracted additional 'considerations,' for example, the greater tax relief given to husbands, based on assumptions regarding gender roles within marriage.

In the traditional marriage 'status contract,' women provide domestic services, care, and sexual services, and men, as heads of families, are responsible for their support (Delphi and Leonard, 1992; Weitzman, 1981). In Okin's (1989) view, it is because the terms of marriage have been fundamentally assumed that they were never enforced, coming into play only when marriage ended. Olsen (1983) has also suggested that state respect for the privacy of the family has been founded on the assumption that there are pre-existing obligations and roles. She cited as evidence the fact that in cases where couples had drawn up explicit contracts (still rare in the early 1980s when she was writing) these contracts had been ignored, something which cannot be explained solely by the state's reluctance to enter the private sphere, which it has been prepared to do since the late nineteenth century (Donzelot, 1980; Gordon, 1988; Lasch, 1977; Lewis, 1984). Even the New Right governments of the 1980s and 1990s, which espoused a philosophy of nonintervention (Mount, 1983), did not hesitate to step in when families demonstrated obvious signs of failure, for example in cases of child abuse.

Thus the assumptions underlying the traditional marriage 'status contract' constructed husbands and wives as equal-but-different partners. The idea of the companionate marriage, which was openly discussed in the interwar period,[1] was based on the complementary nature of the spouses' contributions. Sir William Beveridge's plan for postwar social security arrangements in the United Kingdom was premised on this concept of marriage (E. Wilson, 1977). The basic programs of social protection in Western countries were in large measure built around the labour market and the male worker's relationship to paid work. Women gave less by way of social insurance contributions and received less by way of benefits, generally routed to them via their husbands. This concept of equality as difference was founded on relationships of dependence that mitigated against equal citizenship and resulted in unequal social entitlements. Social insurance in particular operates via the labour market and has always privileged the full-time, usually white, male worker (Gordon, 1990).

In the main, it has always been assumed that the vast majority of the care needed by dependent people will be provided informally by 'the family,' and in particular by women in the family. The idea of a male-breadwinner model family characterized, with varying degrees of accuracy in different countries at different historical moments, the pattern of economic activity in the

---

1 Finch and Summerfield (1991) dated the idea of companionate marriage to the 1940s, but Stone (1979) would put it much earlier than this. Explicit use of the term can be traced to the 1920s (Lindsey and Evans, 1928).

family. In Western countries this model also exercised considerable prescriptive power for much of the twentieth century. Governments assumed that care would be provided by women in stable families, and legislated accordingly. The growing labour market participation of women, together with increased levels of family breakdown, has thus posed major challenges both to family law and the whole structure of social provision. For example, how should the law deal with cohabitation in respect to something like derived pension rights, or, less controversially, responsibility for children? And does more divorce and increased numbers of 'blended families' mean that there is likely to be a larger or a smaller pool of carers for elderly family members?

Changes in Private Law

The reform of private law that took place in the 1960s and 1970s and that introduced 'no-fault' divorce in virtually all Western countries has been widely interpreted as the effective 'deregulation' of the private sphere (Glendon, 1981). This process of liberalization had the effect of allowing men and women, as husbands and wives, to order their own affairs; in other words, it assumed the existence of a degree of individualization. However, husbands and wives are often also parents, and deregulation was neither easy nor successful in regard to parenthood because of the problem of the severe inequalities in unpaid care work, which has secondary effects for women's capacity to achieve self-sufficiency through earnings. As academic research began to sound the alarm about the effects of divorce on children, governments made a renewed effort to regulate the roles of men and women as fathers and mothers. In the United Kingdom, for example, the 1989 Children Act sought to promote 'parental responsibility,' which contained the double meaning of responsibility towards children on the one hand, and a preference for parental responsibility over state responsibility on the other (Eekelaar, 1991). And in 1991, following similar (but better-drafted) attempts in the United States (e.g., Wisconsin) and Australia, the Child Support Act sought to enforce the financial responsibility of fathers for all of their biological children in an effort to make what had been a divorce court decision into an administrative formula.

Having liberalized the law dealing with adult relationships, some attempt had to be made to deal with the problems posed by the care and support of children. In the face of higher levels of family breakdown, the assumption that children would be provided for under the auspices of marriage by men as husbands no longer held, and new ways had to be sought to tie men to their children. The principle articulated in the new child-support legislation was that of biological parenthood, in what may be seen as an effort to construct traditional relationships of support outside marriage (Smart and Neale, 1999). It is not surprising that this initiative failed, given the complicated family lives that people were constructing for themselves (see Chapter 1), which often involved many step-families and social parenthood.

The relaxation of the law relating to divorce took place in Western liberal democracies, where it was neither possible nor desirable to restrict the right to remarry and further reproduce (most often exercised by men). It became supremely difficult to enforce the responsibilities of men in relation to their biological children and, by extension, to those children's carers. The attempt to continue to liberalize family law in respect of adults, while protecting children, also characterized the proposals in the 1990s to increase the role for mediators in divorce. But this did nothing to address the central tensions around the division of unpaid work and resources that bedevilled the issue of providing care and support for children.

Some commentators have demanded that private law go further in recognizing the process of individualization and the changing roles of women in the family. In particular, there has been a call for greater reliance on private ordering via the mechanism of contract, hitherto confined to the public sphere. During the early 1980s there was a burst of powerful criticism of the traditional assumptions underpinning the marriage 'status contract' from American academic feminist lawyers, who observed that the male-breadwinner model no longer matched either the social reality, as vast numbers of married women entered the workforce, or women's aspirations. It seems that many of these critics, like the sociologists of the 1970s, assumed that future behaviour within marriage would become more egalitarian. For example, Weitzman (1981, p. 183) wrote that 'new norms of sharing household responsibility are becoming widely accepted,' and that while men's behaviour had changed more slowly than women's, greater equality in the labour market would in all likelihood be matched in future by greater equality in the home. The views of this influential commentator on family law reflected the ideas of sociologists such as Young and Willmott (1973), with their predictions as to the emergence of 'symmetrical families.' From these observations, feminist legal commentators concluded that more egalitarian decision making in the home could also be expected to emerge.

While patriarchal models of marriage had given way to a companionate ideal, the male-breadwinner model persisted, with the husband as 'head' of the household. For example, in UK social security law this remained formally the case until the implementation of the 1979 European Commission directive on equal treatment. In respect of family law, the feminist answer was to advocate private ordering via contract (Weitzman, 1981) on the assumption that in future marriages would be sufficiently democratic to allow men and women to decide for themselves the precise nature of their commitment. This model of private ordering had much in common with the analysis of greater individualization propounded by both optimists and pessimists in regard to the family (see Chapter 2). Schultz (1982) referred to the existing extensive literature on the realities regarding inequalities of power in marriage (e.g., Safilios Roths-child, 1970, 1976), but argued that in an intimate relationship only those involved could determine what was right for them.

Proponents of a more contractual view of intimate relation-ships acknowledged the greater autonomy and equality of the parties involved and, by shifting the emphasis to private order-ing, sought to provide a new means of securing obligations at a time when family law was perceived to be engaged in a process of deregulation. First, this was a misreading of the role of the state, which, while it was certainly changing in respect of the regulation of adult relationships, was by no means in retreat in respect of the regulation of parents. Second, the problem of obli-gation in personal relationships had in fact much more to do with the gap between the new egalitarian, individualistic model of marital relationships, which was increasingly accepted by governments and inscribed in legislation, and the social realities of marriage and family life, which, as Chapter 1 has shown, con-tinued to be characterized by various dimensions of inequality. Consequently the problem of obligation was unlikely to be solved by contract and private ordering.

Weitzman (1981) and Schultz (1982) hoped that contract would fill the vacuum in family law. Contract relies, after all, on an egal-itarian, individual model of intimate relationships. But contribu-tions by men and women to the family still differ, despite the great increase in female labour market participation. Any idea of private ordering via contract would probably exacerbate this inequality. Schultz (1982) proposed, contrary to the research evidence that has emerged since (Baker and Emry, 1993), that spouses entered marriage knowing the probability of breakdown and that given this, drawing up a contract could only encourage communication between the parties and increase trust. Weitzman (1981) also argued that private ordering by contract was more egalitarian and therefore a better fit with the changing position of women, and that it would promote egalitarian relationships. Much of the feminist sociolegal literature saw contract as both a means of recognizing the more equal roles of men and women in society and as a way of promoting this development. The pragmatic idea that contract was more suited to relationships that were likely to prove temporary was less compelling than the assumption that men and women were now equally ready, able, and willing to negotiate their relationships.

There is, however, a striking capacity of even the well-informed to separate their knowledge about marriage in general from their hopes for their own marriages (Baker and Emry, 1993). Popular reaction to the idea of explicit marriage and cohabitation contracts is often negative. The perception that personal relationships are about more than rational calculation and negotiation, and that their chemistry is too unique, translates into the view of many legal commentators that it is impossible for the intentions of the parties to be known (e.g., Dalton, 1985). Indeed, de Singly (1996) argued that love cannot be contractual because both partners must believe that they are motivated by feelings other than self-interest. Beck and Beck Gernsheim (1995) have also suggested that contracts would result in the secular religion of love losing its mystique and becoming a mixture of market forces and personal impulses. Certainly in the 1990s serious difficulties have been experienced in formalizing the previously informal in the public sphere as contract has been introduced into public sector services (Lewis and Glennerster, 1996). In particular, it has proved difficult to subsume the associational world of the voluntary sector to the rule of contract, which suggests that Karst (1980) and Bellah et al. (1985) may be right in questioning its effects on the world of intimate association. To move to a private contract model for personal relations would in all probability serve to widen the gap between the social reality of personal relationships and the legal assumptions.

Governments in the 1990s have made attempts to create new structures designed to secure private responsibility in the case of child support legislation and private ordering in respect of divorce. But the issue of fairness in the family has not been placed at the top of the agenda for family law reform. The main issue at stake in this regard is the financial welfare of women and children, which is too important a public issue to be left to private ordering or to private responsibility. Okin (1989) has argued further that fairness in the family is sufficiently important to warrant state intervention. Indeed, the importance of this issue is why some proponents want state intervention to make contracts mandatory (Zelig, 1993). But is is often difficult to reconcile people's desire for greater autonomy (which may lie behind the more informal arrangement of cohabitation) and the need for state regulation.

Many ideas have been proposed for establishing a new set of principles to underpin the law of divorce that recognizes rather than denies the problem of inequality between men and women. Some feminists have continued to favour the idea of treating the married couple as a partnership. In this formulation, the concept of property is expanded to include, for example, the human capital represented by the degrees earned by the husband, which may have been made possible by wage earning on the part of the wife (e.g., Weitzman, 1981). Or, more realistically, the idea of a partnership would be recognized by the equal post-divorce sharing of income. Singer (1989) proposed one year of post-divorce income sharing for each two years of marriage. No evidence is provided, though, to support the basis of the formula proposed. Evidence for the scale of losses incurred by women in Britain as a result of childrearing and partial or full absence from the labour market casts doubt on its adequacy (Joshi and Davis, 1992).

Other scholars, feminist and non-feminist, have explored different ideas as to how to recognize the unequal division of paid and unpaid work in households. Eekelaar and Maclean (1986) proposed to compensate a female spouse to the degree that her eventual standard of living after caregiving falls short of what she might have expected had the marriage broken down without caregiving having taken place. In other words, spousal support was to be linked to child support (see also Eekelaar, 1991). Ellman (1989) put forward a non-contractual theory of alimony that encourages 'marital investment.' Alimony is thus conceptualized as an entitlement earned through marital investment. Ellman argued that losses should be equalized, in other words, that the lost earning capacity of the wife that is a consequence of her investment in unpaid work should be recognized. He does not advocate, as have some American traditionalists, a return to fault-based divorce in an effort[2] to secure the male obligation to support (what Smart [1997a] has referred to as the reassertion of public morality).

There is also the issue of whether married couples and cohabitants should be treated in the same way. If there is to be no support for women *qua* women on divorce, then the issues facing policy makers are arguably the same (Hoggett, 1980). However, Deech (1980) maintained that the expectations of those who marry are different from the expectations of those who cohabit. Furthermore, if it is the failure of expectations rather than 'fault' which is the cause of breakdown, then it may be appropriate to continue to distinguish between the two forms of intimate relationship. Much depends on how far people see grounds for making a distinction in cases where there are children. Many jurisdictions do not, and have introduced 'registered partner-

---

2 I say 'effort' because, as many commentators have pointed out, the old law of divorce did not in practice succeed in securing support for women and children.

ships' for cohabitants, including same-sex couples. In handling decisions about how to deal with cohabitation, policy makers have to make explicit their understanding of the concept of 'family.' In most of the Scandinavian countries, social provision is to a large degree individualized. In the Netherlands, all couples and household members are treated equally for the purposes of social security provision, whether they are married or cohabiting, a same-sex couple, or brother and sister. The basic issue is whether they are sharing the costs of supporting a household. But in Germany and the United Kingdom it is fair to say that cohabitants are only treated in the same way as married couples when it is to their financial disadvantage as a couple, and there is strong debate in these countries about how far marriage should be promoted and privileged (Hatland, 2001).

The central problem in all this is an old one: should law be made to treat the social reality, hence recognizing the different contributions of men and women to the family, or should it treat men and women the same? If it does the former, then it risks perpetuating particular gender roles; if it does the latter, then it risks ignoring the reality of women's needs. Family lawyers and policy makers have long been aware of these issues, but their responses have differed markedly over time. In the 1950s, Kahn-Freund (1955, p. 277) argued that social security and maintenance law were more 'realistic than property law because they address the needs of the family rather than the individual.'[3] Like Beveridge (Cmd. 6404, 1942), Kahn-Freund made assumptions about the desirability of the male-breadwinner model for the family. Ellman (1989) in turn has been eager to promote traditional kinds of 'marital investment,' while most feminists have been wary of anything that might encourage women to choose roles that are financially disabling (Kay, 1987). However,

---

3 Kahn-Freund was of course referring to the English law of separate property, developed in the Married Woman's Property Acts between 1870 and 1935.

Fineman (1993, 1994, 1995) has argued, in the manner of Kahn-Freund and Beveridge, that the reality of dependency relationships should be recognized, albeit within a framework that does not rely on marriage or sexual affiliation. American feminists in particular have struggled to identify a set of principles that would establish women's entitlement to resources, rather than a scheme for compensation or financial partnership, given the fact that women's labour is often undervalued (Smith, 1990; Williams, 1994). The search for firm principles as to what might constitute the equal treatment of men and women is extremely difficult, and this approach tends in any case to be at odds with the much more pragmatic one that has operated in the UK jurisdiction, where solicitors generally put the available resources on the table and then divide them with due attention to need and ownership (Jackson et al., 1993).

However, the principles at the heart of the American debate are real and, moreover, have popular appeal in that men and women have shown that they have a strong sense of what might be considered 'fair' treatment of husbands and wives, and mothers and fathers.[4] The underlying problem is that the unpaid work of caring is not equally shared between men and women and that it is not adequately valued. Alimony was traditionally assessed at a low level, not least because the contribution by women in regard to the work of care attracts low wages in the market. The problem is that the debate among American lawyers refers to these huge issues as though they are a matter for private law alone. But there must be limits as to what family law can achieve in this regard. The American debate seeks individualist solutions; but while the obligations of individuals as parents and spouses cannot be ignored, collectivist solutions using the tax system to ensure that children are cared for and

4 The uproar over child support legislation in the United Kingdom provides ample evidence.

supported, and legislation to address the sharing of unpaid work, must also play a part. As the next section shows, moves in some European countries to ensure that men take a greater share of parental leave, and proposals such as that of the Dutch government to encourage a more equal division of unpaid work by encouraging men as well as women to work part-time (Commission on Future Scenarios, 1996), may play a major part in achieving fairness in the family.

This does not mean that family law reform is irrelevant, but only that its limitations must be recognized. Obligation in personal relationships in the context of family change demands both the collective and individual support of children. Britain watered down the child support legislation designed to address the latter; meanwhile the trebling in the number of children in poverty between 1979 and 1991 (Bradshaw, 1997) testifies to the lack of collective support. The problem regarding the support of carers that derives from the gendered division of work also requires attention. This issue has dominated family law debates in the United States but is rarely discussed in the United Kingdom. Fineman (1993, 1994, 1995) in particular has called for the recognition of dependency relationships. Policy in both countries has tended increasingly to recognize individualization and to advocate that all adults, male and female, enter the workforce. But for those caring for children, this can never be more than a partial solution. Yet there is strong evidence that women do not want to be directly dependent on the vagaries of support that follow from dependence on an individual man. Some form of guaranteed maintenance along continental European lines, together with a strong social wage, seems to be a necessary strategy.

Changes in Public Law

The traditional male-breadwinner model was based on a set of assumptions about the stability of marriage and a gendered pattern of contributions at the household level. Female dependence on men was thus inscribed in the model, which was in turn built into the postwar welfare settlement. This model assumed the existence of both regular and full male employment *and* stable families in which women would be provided for largely via their husbands' earnings and social contributions. From its inception, the key program of modern welfare states – social insurance – primarily covered regularly employed male earners; women and children were covered as dependants (Koven and Michel, 1990; Skocpol, 1991; Lewis, 1994). Mothers were not necessarily expected to go out to work. Increasingly the assumptions underlying social policies have moved towards an 'adult worker model family,' in which all adults are assumed to be responsible for their own maintenance, something that appears on the surface to fit with increasing individualization in respect of both family and labour market change. But given that full individualization does not in fact describe the social reality for most countries, this new set of assumptions is bound to pose problems.

Under either set of assumptions about the nature of the family and the way in which it works, lone mothers as a group pose particular problems. As women with children and without men, are they to be treated as mothers or workers? In countries where the male-breadwinner model was strongly embedded in social policies, they tended in the postwar period to be treated as mothers (Lewis, 1997, 1998). Thus in the United Kingdom and the Netherlands lone mothers in receipt of benefits were not required to register for work so long as they had a child under 16. In the United States, too, lone mothers were entitled to claim social assistance benefits. In countries where the male-breadwinner assumptions were rapidly modified, as in Sweden, or were less pervasive, as in France, lone mothers have been less likely to be treated categorically. There is evidence in those countries that adhered to the male-breadwinner-based assumptions longest, and that chose to treat lone mothers as mothers, that there has recently been a shift in attitude towards treating them as workers. This has been most striking in the United Kingdom, the United States and the Netherlands,[5] where governments moved in the mid-1990s towards treating lone mothers in receipt of benefit as workers rather than as mothers. Governments have thus moved towards assuming the existence of an adult rather than a male-breadwinner model. In the United States, the 1996 Personal Responsibility and Work Opportunity Act abolished benefits under the Aid to Families with Dependent Children program (which had become a program serving lone mothers and their children), making 'work first' the order of the day for these women. In the United Kingdom, the Labour government has made the drive from welfare to work central to its social policy since 1997. Tony Blair's introduction to the document on welfare reform has been widely quoted – 'work for those who can; security for those who cannot' (Cm. 3805, 1998, p. iii) – and contrasted with the Beveridgean promise of security for all. The document also made clear that this approach was to apply to women as well as men: 'the welfare state based around the male breadwinner is increasingly out of date' (p. 13).

Several schools of thought have contributed to the profound shift that governments have made in respect of assumptions about the models of work for women that should inform public policy (see, e.g., Lister, 2000). First, a major influence on governments of the early and mid-1990s has been the view that all

5 In Germany, another strong male-breadwinner country, lone mothers have been more likely than married mothers to be employed, but this is largely because the social security system operates differently there. Lone mothers tend to resort to social assistance, which is much less generous than social insurance; they are therefore pushed into the labour market in a way that they are not by the more generous Dutch system of social assistance or by the much less generous, but more gender equal, British system (see Daly, 2000).

those in receipt of state benefits have a concomitant obligation to engage in paid labour. Family change, with the increase in the proportion of lone mother families and their cost to the public purse, has fuelled this line of thought. It seems that individualization makes sense as a principle for policy makers. As more married women entered the labour market, there seemed to many commentators to be little reason why governments should not expect all women, no matter what their circumstances, to be employed.

In the mid-1980s, Lawrence Mead made the case in the United States for the state to assert its moral authority in order to insist that welfare recipients fulfil their obligations as citizens to engage in paid labour. He presented this solution in terms of a model of equal citizenship and something that would bring about greater social integration. Welfare-to-work, implemented first in the United States, embodied these ideas and was applied to all able-bodied adults, lone mothers included. Yet there is much concern on both sides of the Atlantic about 'the family's' capacity and willingness to care and about the quality of care that is given to young and old dependants within it. In the debate over the family, care is lauded and there continues to be mixed feelings about the employment of mothers, especially if they have young children. Care is recognized as important, but the implications of the welfare-to-work agenda have not been confronted. In the United States, prior to the passing of the 1996 Personal Responsibility and Work Opportunities Act, it was openly argued that not only was there a fundamental obligation on the part of able-bodied people to enter the labour market (Mead, 1986), but that it would be better in the case of lone-mother families for the children in those families to have one breadwinner as opposed to none (Novak et al., 1987). In respect of lone-mother families, the American Enterprise Institute arrived at a position roughly similar to that taken by many late Victorians: lone mothers should work but should also be brought into social settings where they might be taught domestic skills (ibid.).

Second, social democrats have, like Mead but unlike more radical critics of 'welfare dependency' (such as Charles Murray), also stressed the overriding importance of employment as a means to social integration or inclusion. The effort to get more lone mothers into the labour market has been justified as much by a desire to improve the welfare of the mothers themselves as by condemnation of welfare dependency. This position is shared by many feminists, who have long stressed the need to recognize the unpaid work of care (Finch and Groves, 1983), but who have also campaigned for women's economic and financial independence (McIntosh, 1981). Welfare-to-work is an idea that has been central to 'Third Way' politics and, as Deacon (1998) has suggested, represents a combination of welfare conceptualized as self-interest, as authority, and as moral regeneration.

Third, globalization and its implications for the whole trajectory of social programs have influenced the thinking of both conservatives and progressives. Conservatives subscribed largely to the neoliberal prescriptions of the Washington Consensus, which dictated private rather than public provision; allocation by markets rather than on the basis of need; targeting rather than universal provision; charging user fees rather than tax-based finance; and decentralization rather than central planning. However, the effects of 'globalization talk' have been more dramatic in terms of the pattern of restructuring of social programs than in cuts to those programs. The demands for competitiveness have bolstered major welfare state services that can be perceived as increasing human capital (chiefly education and health), while at the same time have served to justify a tougher approach to the payment of cash benefits. The call to ensure reciprocity by matching entitlements to benefits with concomitant responsibilities to train or to work is one such approach, although the Labour government's programs in the United Kingdom of a minimum wage and in-work benefits have also been a response to the trade-off between equity and employment that became much more unfavourable for the low-skilled during the 1980s as a result of a low-wage, flexible labour market strategy (Vandenbroucke, 1998).

The globalization thesis directs the attention of government to labour markets and competitiveness. In response the OECD produced a major review of labour strategies in a number of countries in 2000 (OECD, 2000; see also Gough, 1996). European Commission documents also manifest a clear concern about economic competition. The Commission has stressed the importance of adult labour market participation in the context of a strategy to increase European competitiveness (CEC, 1993, 1995). In the economic strategy documents of the Commission, there is little reference to the family and family responsibilities, yet there is obvious concern at the EU level with the work/family nexus, as expressed, for example, in the directive on parental leave (EC96/34). The point is that these two agendas remain parallel and separate and the former predominates. A recent discussion paper issued by the Swedish presidency of the EU acknowledged that 'it will take some time before women's labour market participation matches that of men. ... Unless compensated for, this will leave women at a disadvantage in terms of social protection' (eu2001.se., p. 4), but nevertheless confined its recommendations to improving women's position in the labour market. Thus, greater labour market participation is seen as the best way of securing competitive advantage, of keeping public expenditures down (especially in respect of the growing numbers of lone-mother families), and of promoting social inclusion and reducing poverty.

However, the debate about public policy is not completely dominated by those who stress the importance of adult labour market participation. The recent attention to social capital (see

Chapter 2) was designed to draw attention to the importance of the family and civil society in providing the source of trust and connection crucial to liberal market society. The idea of social capital has been used by some to draw attention to the extent to which no one is an 'unencumbered self' (Sandel, 1996), and to stress interdependence and hence the obligations people have towards one another. However, the solutions favoured by this school of thinking tend to be backward-looking in respect of the family, with a strong hankering after the male-breadwinner model, and to eschew any collective role for the state, which I will argue is necessary if the problems raised by increasing individualization, particularly in respect of reconciling paid and unpaid work, are to be addressed.

Much of the commentary offered by social capital theorists is directed towards reversing the increase in women's employment. But most writers do not go so far as to advocate direct curbs on women's work. Fukuyama (1999) looks to a 'spontaneous re-norming' of society in which women will recognize the importance of staying at home with young children. Similarly, in the United States, Popenoe (1993) expressed the hope that women with children under three will prefer to stay at home (no recompense or supports to enable this to happen are mentioned). Galston (1991, p. 281) has gone further and argued that the liberal state has to take action to protect and promote its distinctive conception of the human good: 'reasonable public arguments for traditionalism' in respect of the family have been, in his view, overlooked. Such arguments in favour of women undertaking more care work are tied to a strong desire to resuscitate the male-breadwinner model family. But, as Iris Marion Young (1995) observed in regard to Galston's proposals, this is effectively to argue that women must be prepared to make themselves dependent on men for the sake of their children and others who may be in need of care.

Feminist work on care has argued that the ethic of care is

based on responsibility and relationship and that there is hence a limit to the extent to which this work can be 'commodified' (Gilligan, 1982; Svenhuijsen, 1998; Baines et al., 1991). Some feminists have gone further and see care as part of an intrinsically female culture and value system that is represented as being of a higher moral order than that of the public sphere (e.g., Elshtain, 1981; Noddings, 1984). This is close to the position of those philosophers who argue that the market and the family are structured by different norms and must therefore be kept separate (Wolfe, 1989; Anderson, 1993). Other feminist writers have concluded that the caring ethic should become the property of men as well as women and that caregivers' rights need to be addressed (Lister, 1997; Tronto, 1993).

This emphasis on care is important in terms of public policy, because the shift towards a set of assumptions based on an adult-worker model does imply a substantially greater commodification of care work, even though this has rarely been made explicit (Esping Andersen, 1999, is an exception). In any case, a large proportion of working women are in low-paid caring jobs as health service workers, social workers, and so on. In the course of the creation of a 'social care market' in Britain since 1993 (Lewis and Glennerster, 1996; Wistow et al., 1996) for example, the conditions of work of many paid carers have deteriorated. Early work by Scandinavian feminists suggested that the process by which women in those countries had been drawn into the labour market to carry out care work in the public sector since the 1970s amounted to a form of public as opposed to private patriarchy (Siim, 1987). Later, Scandinavian feminists became more optimistic about the possibilities of a 'women-friendly' state (Hernes, 1987). However, for the most part care jobs in the English-speaking countries are characterized by poor wages and working conditions, especially for part-time workers. In the United Kingdom in the 1990s, many policy makers advocating the 'New Deal' program designed to encourage lone parents to seek employment expected that lone mothers would find jobs in the formal care sector.

During the late 1990s a relatively coherent set of supply-side changes, which some have labelled the 'Third Way,' could be observed in many western European countries. Thus, Green-Pedersen et al. (2001) suggested that active labour market policies, job creation, the promotion of high rates of labour market participation, macro-economic stability, and wage moderation have characterized policies in both Denmark and the Netherlands. A similar picture can be drawn for the United Kingdom since 1997 (Glennerster, 1999; Lewis, 1999). Broadly speaking, there is evidence that the relationship between paid work and welfare, which has been central to the development of twentieth-century welfare states, is being reworked, with the emphasis on activity; that is, on paid work, rather than on so-called passive benefits.

Such an adult-worker model is not necessarily bad for women. Everything depends on the conditions under which such a model is implemented. The problems of assuming the existence of a full adult-worker model are fourfold:

- Unpaid care work is unequally shared between men and women, which has important implications for women's position in the labour market.
- Given the lack of good quality affordable care in the formal sector (public or private) in most countries, many women have little option but to continue to provide care.
- Many female carers feel a moral obligation to prioritize care over paid work.
- Women's low pay, especially in care-related jobs, means that full individualization is hard to achieve on the basis of long part-time or even full-time work.

Just as policy assumptions based on the old male-breadwinner model disadvantaged women in particular, assumptions based on a full adult-worker model are also likely to do so. Any assumption that wages will enable more self-provision in the social arena, especially in respect of pensions, is fraught with danger for women. The new welfare contract in Western countries is moving increasingly from social contributions to individually defined contributions, premised on equal participation in the workforce, but this is an unrealistic assumption in respect of women. Assumptions regarding an adult-worker model pose threats to women unless issues to do with the unequal gendered division of work and hence of lifetime earnings are addressed.

It is therefore necessary to look more closely at the balance between paid and unpaid work. The Scandinavian countries and the United States provide useful models in this regard. Both have developed a fully individualized, adult-worker model. However, in the US case, the obligation to enter the labour market is embedded in a residual welfare system that often borders on the punitive, whereas in Sweden and Denmark it is supported by an extensive range of care entitlements in respect of children and older people. The position of lone mothers – always a border case for the study of public policy – is instructive in this respect because for them the problem of combining unpaid care work and employment is particularly acute. The United States has gone much more wholeheartedly than Britain down the road of treating these women as paid workers, imposing time-limited benefits. Employment rates of lone mothers are high in the United States; the push factor is strong. But employment rates are higher still in Sweden and Denmark and lone mothers' poverty rates are much lower than in the United Kingdom or the United States. Indeed, Sweden comes closest to having achieved Mead's ideal in which all adult citizens are obliged to engage in paid work in order to qualify for a wide range of benefits, which then permit them to leave the labour market for cause (e.g., as carers for young children). However, Swedish lone mothers still get one-third of their income from the state (Lewis, 1998). The system is based on a commitment to universal citizenship entitlements, rather than, as in the United States, a grafting of equal citizenship obligations on to a residual welfare model.

Put simply, the Scandinavian adult-worker model has recognized care and hence practises what White (2000) has called 'fair reciprocity.' All able-bodied adults are treated as citizen-workers, yet permission to exit the labour market in order to care with wage replacement is granted, and formal care services are provided. In effect, Sweden and Denmark's individualized model is similar to the US model, but their systems have the capacity to compensate for the difference that manifests itself in the form of an unequal division of care work (Lewis and Astrom, 1992). The family penalty experienced by female carers is less than that in most other countries, although there is still a penalty to be paid for moving between paid and unpaid work; Sweden has one of the most sexually segregated labour markets in the Western world, which brings us back to the problem of the unequal division of care work. In any case, until men do more care work, in all probability it will not be valued any more highly.

Whether care is paid or unpaid it cannot be understood simply in terms of activity, tasks, or tending. Love and duty are strong factors in the gendering of care work. The obligation to care is generally felt more powerfully by women than by men, which explains why women have tended to add their increasing hours of paid work onto unpaid care work. However, it is the understanding of care as a process, human activity, and moral orientation that makes it possible to challenge the policy-making discourse and to seek 'equal billing' for care in the policy debate. The literature devoted to developing an ethic of care proposes an alternative model of relationship and connection, and makes a strong case for enabling all human beings to care. While the arguments for and against full individualization, together with the policy trend towards the implementation of an adult-worker model, signal the importance of treating care as work in order to properly value it, the arguments that take a care-centred perspective highlight the importance of the valuation and the redistribution of care work.

Amartya Sen's (1987) work on 'capabilities' provides a means of addressing care work, which the concepts of poverty and social exclusion tend to close off. Sen has defined capabilities as combinations of functionings from which an individual can choose. They apply to political and social life as well as life in the family. The concept thus embraces more than material well-being, wages, and paid work. Building on Sen's work, Meghnad Desai's (2000) analysis of well-being has drawn attention to the importance of 'social goods,' provided jointly by a household or a group, and the time and labour involved in their production.

Unpaid care work is shared unequally between men and women, and this has serious implications for women's position in the labour market. Given the lack of good-quality, affordable care in the formal sector, many women have little option but to continue to provide it informally (Land and Rose [1985] referred to this as 'compulsory altruism') and to depend to some extent on a male wage. Nevertheless, a significant number of female carers feel that it is 'right' to prioritize care. Whether they would want to do so if good-quality, affordable child care services became widely available remains an open question. Men currently do not have the opportunity to prioritize care work. Creighton (1999) has concluded that policies to address the issue of sharing work, paid and unpaid, are vital. At the supranational level, almost a decade ago the OECD (1991) promoted the idea of combining work and care for men and women. (A policy along this line was promoted by the Netherlands with its 'Combination Scenario' put together by the Minister of Social Affairs' Committee for Future Scenarios, but it was inadequately implemented [Plantenga et al., 1999]).

Policies based on an ethic of care must be attentive to how that care is shared. It is important that both men and women have the possibility of genuine choice, and that women can also choose employment, especially given that their welfare increasingly depends on their own efforts. Care policies may promote the traditional division of labour associated with the male-breadwinner model or they may promote a more equal division of labour. Conservative and communitarian commentators tend to favour cash allowances as a means of recognizing care (Morgan, 1995). Thus Coleman (1993, 1995) advocated 'bounties' that would compensate 'parents'[6] for the costs of child care and reward good child-rearing outcomes. Cash benefits and allowances are often promoted as a means of permitting women greater choice as to whether to care at home, or to hire a carer and work outside the home. In practice, the choice is usually a figment, because the costs of choosing one option over another are not equal.

The provision of care services in the formal sector tends to work in the reverse direction, providing paid employment for women and allowing female carers to enter the labour market. Bradshaw et al.'s (1996) cross-national study of lone mothers' employment showed affordable child care to be the key variable explaining the differences in employment rates between the countries. But accessibility and quality are also important. In fact, genuine choice between care work and employment requires the provision of both cash and services. In respect of children under school age, to carry on working, a carer requires good child-care services, which even in EU countries are available only in the Scandinavian countries, Italy, France, and Belgium. To have a genuine option of taking parental leave, the carer must be able to return to her job and to receive cash compensation at a high replacement level. Furthermore, if care is to be shared and the capacities for caring work are to be developed

---

6 Strangely, Coleman (1995) denied that his scheme carries any gender implications.

for all human beings, then men must be allowed to take leave and be recompensed. In Norway and Sweden part of parental leave is reserved for the father and is lost if he does not take it. Of children born in 1995, 77 per cent had fathers who used the whole month of leave, although fathers still take much less leave than mothers overall (Bjornberg, 2002). A policy such as parental leave can be implemented so that it promotes female labour market exit, as in Germany, or as a way of promoting greater gender equality in respect of paid and unpaid work (Bruning and Plantenga, 1999).

Anything to do with care tends to be poorly valued. Wages in the formal sector are low, and benefits and allowances for carers in the informal sector are also low. This means that, in a world in which individualization and the capacity for self-provisioning are increasingly being expected by policy makers, carers are profoundly disadvantaged. It also means that care continues to be associated with women rather than with both the sexes (Leira, 1998). For example, the German social care insurance scheme in respect of adult dependants offers elderly people services or a cash payment, and apparently most claimants choose the latter and then route the money through to the female carers who have hitherto been providing care on an unpaid basis (Evers, 1998). It is hard to say whether this outcome is a positive step towards recognizing unpaid care work, or a policy that reinforces women's traditional responsibilities.

Thus far, recent approaches to welfare by policy makers and academics (e.g., Esping Andersen, 2000) have focused on the need for reforms to secure changes to the social security system that will promote labour market entry. But given the unequal division of paid and unpaid work and the responsibility to care, it is also important that reform and restructuring take into account people's lifetime relationships to the labour market, for example in respect of pension guarantees. Carers are particularly prone to low-paid work and periods with no pay.

In a world where dignity as well as welfare in the broadest sense derives mainly from wages, it is crucial that care is valued. Some fear that commodification will undermine the motivation that inspires care (Himmelweit, 1995). But if care work is not valued it is degraded and exploitative. A strong argument has been made that gender justice requires the proper valuation of care (Bubeck, 1995; Nelson, 1999). It must be recognized that care work has to be done. While birth rates are falling in many countries, the proportion of frail elderly people is increasing. Those aged 85 and over are projected to be three times more numerous in 2050 in the United Kingdom, where the projected dependency ratio is not as unfavourable as in many other countries, Canada included (see Table 14), than now (Cm. 4192, 1999, para. 2.19). Governments that adopt an adult-worker model while ignoring the provision of care are headed on a perilous course. Without access to affordable, good-quality support for care, women may resist the injunction to full individualization so far as they are able, or substantial hardship may be visited on dependants, young and old.

Public policy could help realize a more coherent and integrated set of principles on care by remedying its own dichotomized approach to paid and unpaid work and by promoting the rethinking of principles underlying social provision such that the gender inequalities in the division of work and lifetime earnings are addressed. Given the existence of what is in most countries a one-and-a-half earner rather than a fully fledged adult-worker model, more attention has to be paid to policies that:

- Provide compensation for care and encourage more equal sharing between men and women of the unpaid care work that all societies need.
- Regulate the hours of paid employment.

- Promote the redistribution of and transitions between different types of work, paid and unpaid, over the life course.

There is also the need to provide life-chance guarantees for those (men as well as women) entering low-paid flexible jobs (often in human services), so that they have the chance to leave them and so that those staying in them are compensated (Esping Andersen, 2000). Assumptions regarding the existence of the male-breadwinner model historically were embedded in social insurance welfare systems. As these are called into question by family change and by the increasing flexibilization of men's as well as women's work, society faces the major challenge of fundamentally rethinking the building blocks of social provision. The danger is that new assumptions regarding an adult-worker model will support a move towards an individual contractualism under private law and in public policy that overestimates women's economic independence and capacity to self-provision, and insists on an unfair reciprocity that ignores care work.

Margrit Eichler (1997) sketched out three different models of the family that may underpin family policies: the patriarchal family, premised on the notion of separate spheres for men and women and resulting in the most extreme form of gender inequality; the individual responsibility model of the family, in which men and women are assumed to take equal responsibility for economic and care contributions in families, but do so in the absence of any collective supports; and the social responsibility model, in which the public shares responsibility with parents for the care of dependants. The English-speaking world still operates primarily in accordance with the individual responsibility model; continental European countries have tended to offer many more examples of the exercise of social responsibility. In response to what has been dramatic family change and sustained change in the economic contributions that women make to families, the response in the English-speaking countries has been considerable anxiety about the decline of the traditional two-parent, male-breadwinner family. But there has nevertheless been a movement to build on the trend towards ever-increasing individualization in terms of making a new set of assumptions about men's and women's equal capacities to work, and to share and negotiate their responsibilities as parents. Such an approach is most evident in the United States and, to use Skocpol's (2000) term, amounts to a 'missing middle' so far as policy is concerned. Better-off parents can buy care in the market for children (or elderly dependants), but the struggle to combine work and care is particularly harsh for poorer families, for both working adults and young and old dependants. The example of many of the continental European countries shows that the choice does not have to be between an unsupported adult-worker model family and a traditional male-breadwinner family. Few women would wish to go back to being housewives and for a majority of families it is not in any case an economically viable choice. But care requires support. There are many ways of doing this: via collective provision, policies that address working hours, and policies that attempt to change the allocation of resources (time and money) within households. Various continental European countries have put these forms of support together differently, but what they have in common is a recognition that the massively changed circumstances of family form and family life require public policies for care.

References

Adams, M.A. (1998). 'How Does Marriage Matter? Individuation and Institutionalization in the Trajectory of Gendered Relationships.' Unpublished paper, ASA Conference, 21–5 August, San Francisco.

Akerloff, G.A. (1998). 'Men without Children.' *Economic Journal* 108 (March): 287–309.

Alwin, D.F., Braun, M., and Scott, J. (1992). 'The Separation of Work and the Family: Attitudes towards Women's Labour-Force Participation in Britain, Germany and the United States.' *European Sociological Review* 8: 13–38.

Anderson, E. (1993). *Value in Ethics and Economics*. Cambridge, Mass.: Harvard University Press.

Arber, S., and Ginn, J. (1991). *Gender and Later Life*. London: Sage.

Arber, S., and Ginn, J. (1995). 'The Mirage of Gender Equality: Occupational Success in the Labor Market and within Marriage.' *British Journal of Sociology* 46(1): 21–43.

Baines, C., Evans, P., and Neysmith, S. (1991). *Women's Caring: Feminist Perspectives on Social Welfare*. Toronto: McClelland and Stewart.

Baker, L., and Emry, R. (1993). 'When Every Relationship Is above Average: Perceptions and Expectations of Divorce at the Time of Marriage.' *Law and Human Behavior* 17 (4): 439–50.

Bane, M.J. (1976). *Here to Stay: American Families in the Twentieth Century.* New York: Basic Books.

Bane, M.J., and Jargowsky, P.A. (1988). 'The Links between Government Policy and Family Structure: What Matters and What Doesn't.'

In A. Cherlin (ed.), *The Changing American Family and Public Policy.* Washington, DC: Urban Institute Press.

Barrett, M., and McIntosh, M. (1982). *The Anti-Social Family.* London Verso.

Bauman, Z. (1993). *Postmodern Ethics.* Oxford: Blackwell.

Bauman, Z. (1995). *Life in Fragments.* Oxford: Blackwell.

Beaujot, R. (2000). *Earning and Caring in Canadian Families.* Peterborough, Ont.: Broadview Press.

Beck, U., and Beck Gernsheim, E. (1995). *The Normal Chaos of Love.* Cambridge: Polity Press.

Beck Gernsheim, E. (1999). 'On the Way to a Post-Familial Family: From a Community of Need to Elective Affinities.' *Theory, Culture and Society* 15 (3–4): 53–70.

Becker, G. (1981). *A Treatise on the Family.* Cambridge, Mass.: Harvard University Press.

Becker, G., Landes, E.M., and Michael, R.T. (1977). 'An Economic Analysis of Marital Instability.' *Journal of Political Economy* 85 (61): 1141–87.

Bellah, R., Madsen R., Sullivan, W., Swidler, A., and Tipton, S.M. (1985). *Habits of the Heart: Middle America Observed.* Berkeley: University of California Press.

Berger, P., and Kellner, H. (1964). 'Marriage and the Construction of Reality.' *Diogenes* (46): 1–25.

Berger, B., and Berger, P.L. (1983). *The War over the Family: Capturing the Middle Ground.* London: Hutchinson.

Bernard, J. (1976). *The Future of Marriage.* Harmondsworth: Penguin.

Bjornberg, U. (2002). 'Ideology and Choice between Work and Care: Swedish Policy for Working Parents.' *Critical Social Policy* 22 (1): 33–52.

Booth, C. (1892). *Life and Labour of the People in London*, vols. 1–8. London: Macmillan.

Bosanquet, H. (1906). *The Family.* London: Macmillan.

Bradshaw, J. et al. (1996). *Lone Mothers and Work.* Findings no. 96, York: Joseph Rowntree Foundation.

Bradshaw, J. (1997). 'Child Welfare in the UK: Rising Poverty, Falling Priorities for Children.' In C.A. Cornia and S. Danziger (eds.), *Child Poverty and Deprivation in the Industrialized Countries, 1945–1995.* Oxford: Clarendon Press.

Brody, E. (1981). '"Women in the Middle" and Family Help to Older People.' *The Gerontologist* 21: 471–80.

Bruning, G., and Plantenga, J. (1999). 'Parental Leave and Equal Opportunities: Experiences in Eight European Countries.' *Journal of European Social Policy* 9 (3): 195–209.

Bubeck, D. (1995). *Care, Gender and Justice.* Oxford: Clarendon Press.

Bundesanstalt für Arbeit. (1999). *Arbeitsmarkt 1998: Amtliche Nachrichten der Bundesanstalt für Arbeit,* Nürnberg: Author.

Burgess, E.W., and Locke, H.J. (1953). *The Family from Institution to Companionship* (2nd ed.). New York: American Book Co.

Burns, A., and Scott, C. (1994). *Mother-Headed Families and Why They Have Increased.* New Jersey: Lawrence Erlbaum.

Cancian, F.M. (1987). *Love in America: Gender and Self-Development.* Cambridge: Cambridge University Press.

CEC. (1993). *Growth, Competitiveness and Employment – The Challenges and Ways forward into the 21st Century.* Luxembourg: CEC.

CEC. (1995). *Equal Opportunities for Women and Men – Follow-up to the White Paper on Growth, Competitiveness and Employment.* Brussels: DGV.

Cheal, D. (1991). *Family and the State of Theory.* Hemel Hempstead: Harvester Wheatsheaf.

Cherlin, A. (1981). *Marriage, Divorce and Remarriage.* Cambridge, Mass.: Harvard University Press.

Cherlin, A. (1992). *Marriage, Divorce, Remarriage* (2nd ed.). Cambridge, Mass.: Harvard University Press.

Chester, R. (1971). 'Contemporary Trends in the Stability of English Marriage.' *Journal of Biosocial Science* 3: 389–402.

Clarkberg, M., Stolzenberg, R.M., and Waite, L.J. (1995). 'Attitudes, Values, and Entrance into Cohabitational versus Marital Unions.' *Social Forces* 74 (2): 609–34.

Cmd. 6404. (1942). *Report of the Committee on Social Insurance and Allied Services. London:* HMSO.

Cmd. 5629. (1974). *Report of the Committee on One-Parent Families.* London: HMSO.

Cmnd. 8173. (1982). *Growing Older.* London: HMSO.

Cm. 3805. (1998). *New Ambitions for Our Country: A New Contract for Welfare.* London: The Stationery Office.

Cm. 41921–I. (1999). *With Respect to Old Age: Report of the Royal Commission on Long-Term Care*. London: The Stationery Office.

Cohen, L. (1987). 'Marriage, Divorce, and Quasi Rents; or, "I gave him the best years of my life."' *Journal of Legal Studies* 16 (2): 267–304.

Coleman, D., and Chandola, T. (1999). 'Britain's Place in Europe's Population.' In S. McRae (ed.), *Changing British Families and Household in the 1990s*. Oxford: Oxford University Press.

Coleman, J.S. (1988). 'Social Capital in the Creation of Human Capital.' *American Journal of Sociology* 94 (Suppl.): S95–S120.

Coleman, J.S. (1993). 'The Rational Reconstruction of Society.' *American Sociological Review* 58: 1–15.

Coleman, J.S. (1995). 'Rights and Interests: Raising the Next Generation.' *American Soicological Review* 60: 782–3.

Commission on Future Scenarios for the Redistribution of Unpaid Work. (1996). *Shared Care*. The Hague: Author.

Coontz, S. (1991). *The Way We Never Were: American Families and the Nostalgia Trap*. New York: Basic Books.

Cooper, D. (1972). *The Death of the Family*. Harmondsworth: Penguin.

Creighton, C. (1999). 'The Rise and Decline of the "Male Breadwinner Family" in Britain.' *Cambridge Journal of Economics* 23: 519–41.

Crompton, R. (ed.). (1999). *Restructuring Gender Relations and Employment: The Decline of the Male Breadwinner*. Oxford: Oxford University Press.

Dalton, C. (1985). 'An Essay in the Deconstruction of Contract Doctrine.' *Yale Law Journal* 94 (5): 997–1114.

Daly, M. (2000). *The Gender Division of Welfare*. Cambridge: Cambridge University Press.

Davis, K. (1985). 'The Future of Marriage.' In K. Davis (ed.), *Contemporary Marriage*. New York: Russell Sage Foundation.

Deacon, A. (1998). 'The Green Paper on Welfare Reform: A Case for Enlightened Self-Interest?' *Political Quarterly* 69 (3): 306–11.

Deech, R. (1980). 'The Case against Legal Recognition of Cohabitation.' In J.M. Eekelaar and S.N. Katz (eds.). *Marriage and Cohabitation in Contemporary Societies*. Toronto: Butterworths.

Delphi, C., and Leonard, C. (1992). *Familiar Exploitation: A New Analysis of Marriage in Contemporary Western Society*. Cambridge: Polity Press.

Dench, G. (1994). *The Frog, the Prince and the Problem of Men*. London: Neanderthal Books.

Dennis, N., and Erdos, G. (1992). *Families without Fatherhood*. London: IEA.

Desai, M. (2000). 'Well being or wel fare?.' In N. Fraser and J. Hills (eds.), *Public Policy for the 21st Century.* Social and Economic Essays in Memory of Henry Neuburger. Bristol: Policy Press

Despert, L. (1953). *Children of Divorce*. New York: Doubleday.

Donzelot, J. (1980). *The Policing of Families*. London: Hutchinson.

Edgeworth, F.Y. (1922). 'Equal Pay to Men and Women for Equal Work. *Economic Journal* 32: 453–7.

Eekelaar, J. (1991). *Regulating Divorce*. Oxford: Clarendon

Eekelaar, J., and Maclean, M. (1986). *Maintenance after Divorce*. Oxford: Clarendon Press.

Ehrenreich, B. (1983). *The Hearts of Men: American Dreams and the Flight from Commitment*. London: Pluto Press.

Eichler, M. (1997). *Family Shifts: Families Policies and Gender Equality*. Oxford: Oxford University Press.

Elias, N. (1991). *The Society of Individuals*. Oxford: Blackwell.

Ellman, I.M. (1989). 'The Theory of Alimony.' *California Law Review* 77 (1): 3–81

Ellwood, D., and Bane, M.J. (1985). 'The Impact of AFDC on Family Structure and Living Arrangements.' In R.G. Ehrenberg (ed.), *Research in Labor Economics* (Vol. 7). Greenwich, Conn: JAI Press.

Elshtain, J.B. (1981). *Public Man, Private Woman: Women in Social and Political Thought*. Princeton: Princeton University Press.

Ermisch, J., and Francesconi, M. (2000). 'Patterns of Household and Fund Foundation.' In R. Berthoud and R. Ermisch (eds.), *Seven Years in the Lives of British Families*. Bristol: Policy Press.

Ermisch, J., and Francesconi, M. (1998). *Cohabitation in Great Britain: Not for Long, but Here to Stay*, WP 98–1. University of Essex: ESRC Research Centre on Micro-Social Change.

Ermisch, J., and Francesconi, M. (2001). *The Effect of Parents' Employment on Children's Lives*. London: Family Policy Studies Centre.

Esping Andersen, G. (1999). *Social Foundations of Postindustrial Economies*. Oxford: Oxford University Press.

Esping Andersen, G. (2000). 'Challenge to the Welfare State in the

21st Century: Ageing Societies, Knowledge Based Economies and the Sustainability of European Welfare States.' Paper presented to the conference 'Comparer les Systèmes de Protection Sociale en Europe, Ministère de L'Emploi et de la Solidarité, Paris, 8 and 9 June.

Eu2001.se. 'Gender Equality and Social Security: An Engine for Economic Growth.' Presidency Discussion Paper. Stockholm: EC.

Evers, A. (1998). 'The New Long Term Care Insurance Policy in Germany.' *Journal of Aging and Social Policy* 10 (1): 77–97.

Finch, J., and Groves, D. (eds.). (1983). *Labour and Love: Women, Work and Caring*. London: Routledge and Kegan Paul.

Finch, J., and Mason, J. (1993). *Negotiating Family Responsibilities*. London: Tavistock/Routledge.

Finch, J., and Summerfield, P. (1991). 'Social Reconstruction and the Emergence of Companionate Marriage.' In D. Clark (ed.). *Marriage, Domestic Life and Social Change: Writings for Jacqueline Burgoyne, 1944–1988*. London: Routledge.

Fineman, M.A. (1993). 'Our Sacred Institution: The Ideal of the Family in American Law and Society.' *Utah Law Review* (2): 387–405.

Fineman, M.A. (1994). 'The End of Family Law? Intimacy in the Twenty-First Century.' In S. Ingber (ed.), *Changing Perspectives of the Family, Proceedings of the 5th Annual Symposium of the Constitutional Law Resource Center*. Des Moines: Drake University Law School.

Fineman, M.A. (1995). *The Neutered Mother, the Sexual Family and Other Twentieth Century Tragedies*. London: Routledge.

Fletcher, R. (1966). *The Family and Marriage in Britain*. Harmondsworth: Penguin.

Fukuyama, F. (1999). *The Great Disruption: Human Nature and the Reconstitution of Social Order*. London: Profile Books.

Furstenberg, F.F. and Cherlin, A.J. (1991). *Divided Families. What Happens to Children When Parents Part*. Cambridge Mass.: Harvard University Press.

Galston, W. (1991). *Liberal Purposes, Good Virtues and Diversity in the Liberal State*. Cambridge: Cambridge University Press.

Gergen, K.J. (1991). *The Saturated Self: Dilemmas of Identity in Contemporary Life*. New York: Basic Books.

Gershuny, J. (2000). *Changing Times: Work and Leisure in Post-Industrial Society.* Oxford: Oxford University Press.

Giddens, A. (1992). *The Transformation of Intimacy: Sexuality, Love and Eroticism in Modern Societies.* Cambridge: Polity.

Gilder, G. (1981). *Wealth and Poverty.* New York: Basic Books.

Gilder, G. (1987). 'The Collapse of the American Family.' *The Public Interest* (Fall): 20–5.

Gilligan, C. (1982). *In a Different Voice.* Cambridge, Mass. Harvard University Press.

Gillis, J.R. (1986). *For Better, for Worse: British Marriages, 1600 to the Present.* Oxford: Oxford University Press.

Gillis, J. (1997). *A World of Their Own Making. A History of Myth and Ritual in Family Life.* Oxford: Oxford University Press.

Ginzberg, L. (1990). *Women and the Work of Benevolence.* New Haven: Yale University Press.

Glendon, M.A. (1981). *The New Family and the New Property.* Toronto: Butterworths.

Glenn, N.D. (1987). 'Continuity versus Change, Sanguineness versus Concern: Views of the American Family in the Late 1980s.' *Journal of Family Issues* 8 (4): 348–54.

Glennerster, H. (1999). 'Which Welfare States Are Most Likely to Survive?' *International Journal of Social Welfare* 8: 2–11.

Goldstein, J., Freud, A., and Solnit, A. (1980). *Beyond the Best Interests of the Child.* London: Burnett Books.

Goldthorpe, J.H., Lockwood, D, Beckhofer, F., and Platt, J. (1969). *The Affluent Worker: Industrial Attitudes and Behaviour.* Cambridge: Cambridge University Press.

Goode, W. (1956). *After Divorce.* Glencoe, Ill.: Free Press.

Gordon, L. (1988). *Heroes of Their Own Lives: The Politics and History of Family Violence in Boston, 1880–1960.* New York: Viking.

Gordon, L. (ed.). (1990). *Women, The State and Welfare.* Madison: University of Wisconsin Press.

Gough, I. (1996). 'Social Welfare and Competitiveness.' *New Political Economy* 1 (2): 209–32.

Green-Pedersen, C., van Kersbergen, K., and Hemmerijke, A. (2001). 'Neo-liberalism, the 'Third Way' or What? Recent Social Democratic

Welfare Policies in Denmark and The Netherlands.' *Journal of European Public Policy* 8 (2): 307–25.

Griffiths, M. (1995). *Feminisms and the Self: The Web of Identity.* London: Routledge.

Hakim, C. (1996). *Key Issues in Women's Work: Female Heterogeneity and the Polarization of Women's Employment.* London: Athlone.

Hakim, C. (2000). *Work-Lifestyle Choices in the Twenty-first Century: Preference Theory.* Oxford: Oxford University Press.

Hall, D.R. (1996). 'Marriage as a Pure Relationship: Exploring the Link between Pre-marital Cohabitation and Divorce in Canada.' *Journal of Comparative Family Studies* 27 (1): 1–12.

Haller, M., and Hoellinger, F. (1994). 'Female Employment and the Change of Gender Roles: The Conflictual Relationship between Participation and Attitudes in International Comparison.' *International Sociology* 9 (1): 87–112.

Halsey, A.H. (1993). 'Changes in the Family.' *Children and Society* 7 (2): 125–36.

Harkness, S., Machin, S., and Waldfogel, J. (1996). 'Women's Pay and Family Incomes in Britain, 1979–91.' In J. Hills (ed.), *New Inequalities: The Changing Distribution of Incomes and Wealth in the UK,* Cambridge: Cambridge University Press.

Hartland, A. (2001). 'Changing Family Patterns: A Challenge to Social Security.' In M. Kautto, J. Fritzell, B. Hvinden, J. Kvist, and H. Uusitalo (eds.), *Nordic Welfare States in the European Context.* London: Routledge.

Haskey, J. (1995). 'Trends in Marriage and Cohabitation: The Decline in Marriage and the Changing Pattern of Living in Partnerships.' *Population Trends* (80): 5–15.

Haskey, J. (1999). 'Cohabitation and Marital Histories of Adults in Great Britain.' *Population Trends* (96, Summer): 1–12.

Held, V. (1993). *Feminist Morality: Transforming Culture, Society and Politics.* Chicago: University of Chicago Press.

Henley Centre (1999). *The Paradox of Prosperity.* London: Henley Centre and the Salvation Army.

Hernes, H. (1987). *The Welfare State and Woman Power.* Oslo: Norwegian University Press.

Hetherington, E., Cox, M., and Cox, R. (1978). 'The Aftermath of

Divorce.' In J. Stevens and M. Matthews (eds.), *Mother-Child, Father-Child Relations*. Washington, DC: National Association for the Education of Young Children.

Himmelweit, S. (1995). 'The Discovery of "Unpaid Work": The Social Consequences of the Expansion of "Work."' *Feminist Economics* 1 (2).: 1–19.

Hoggett, B. (1980). 'Ends and Means: The Utility of Marriage as a Legal Institution.' In J.M. Eekelaar and S.N. Katz (eds.), *Marriage and Cohabitation in Contemporary Societies*. Toronto: Butterworths.

Hooghiemstra, E. (1997). 'Een- en tweeverdieners.' In M. Niphuis-Nell (ed.), *Sociale Atlas van de Vrouw, deel 4: Veranderingen in de Primaire Leefsfeer*, Rijswijk: Sociaal en Cultureel Planbureau.

Howard, M. (1993). 'Picking up the Pieces.' Mimeo, presented at Conservative Political Centre Fringe Meeting, Blackpool, 5 October.

Inglehart, R. (1997). *Culture Shift in Advanced Industrial Society*. Princeton: Princeton University Press.

Jackson, E. et al. (1993). 'Financial Support in Divorce: The Right Mixture of Rules and Discretion.' *International Journal of Law and the Family* 7: 230–54.

Jarvis, H., (1997). 'Housing, Labour Markets and Household Structure: Questioning the Role of Secondary Data Analysis in Sustaining the Polarization Debate.' *Regional Studies* 31 (5): 521–31.

Joshi, H., and Davis, H. (1992). *Child Care and Mothers' Lifetime Earnings: Some European Contrasts*. London: Centre for Economic Policy Research.

Joshi, H., and Verropoulou, G. (2000). *Maternal Employment and Child Outcomes. Analysis of Two Birth Cohort Studies*. London: Smith Institute.

Kahn-Freund, O. (1955). 'England.' In W. Friedmann (ed.), *Matrimonial Property Law*. London: Stevens and Sons.

Karst, K.L. (1980). 'The Freedom of Intimate Association.' *Yale Law Journal* 89 (1): 624–92.

Kay, H.H. (1987). 'Equality and Difference: A Perspective on No-Fault Divorce and Its Aftermath.' *University of Cincinnati Law Review* 56 (1): 1–90.

Keuzekamp, S., and K. Oudhof (2000). *Emancipatiemonitor*. Den Haag: Sociaal en Cultureel Planbureau.

Kiernan, K. (1992). 'The Impact of Family Disruption in Childhood on Transitions Made in Young Adult Life.' *Population Studies* 46: 213–34.

Kiernan, K. (1999). 'Cohabitation in Western Europe.' *Population Trends* 96 (Summer): 25–32.

Kiernan, K. (2000). 'Cohabitation in Western Europe: Trends, Issues and Implications.' Paper present at the Family Issues Symposium, Population Research Institute, Pennsylvania State University.

Kiernan, K., Land, H., and Lewis, J. (1998). *Lone Motherhood in Twentieth-Century Britain*. Oxford: Oxford University Press.

Kotlikoff, L. (1992). *Generational Accounting: Knowing Who Pays, and When, for What We Spend*. New York: The Free Press.

Koven, S., and Michel, S. (1990). 'The Most Womanly of Women's Duties: Maternalist Politics and the Emergence of Welfare States, 1880–1920.' *American Historical Review* 95: 1076–108.

Kuijsten, A. C. (1996). 'Changing Family Patterns in Europe: A Case of Divergence?' *European Journal of Population* 12 (2): 115–43.

Land, H. (1980). 'The Family Wage.' *Feminist Review* (5): 55–77.

Land, H., and Rose, H. (1985). 'Compulsory Altruism for Some or an Altruistic Society for All?' In P. Bean, J. Ferris, and D. Whynes (eds.), *In Defence of Welfare*. London: Tavistock.

Larkin, P. (1988). 'This Be the Verse.' In *Collected Poems*. London: Faber and Faber.

Lasch, C. (1977). *Haven in a Heartless World*. New York: Basic Books.

Laurie, H., and Gershuny, J. (2000). 'Couples, Work and Money.' In R. Berthoud and J. Gershuny (eds.), *Seven Years in the Lives of British Families*. Bristol: The Policy Press.

Lawson, A. (1988). *Adultery. An Analysis of Love and Betrayal*. Oxford: Blackwell.

Leach, E. (1967). *A Runaway World?* Oxford: Oxford University Press.

Leira, A. (1998). 'Caring as Social Right: Cash for Child Care and Daddy Leave.' *Social Politics* 5 (3): 362–79.

Lesthaeghe, R. (1995). 'The Second Demographic Transition in Western Countries: An Interpretation.' In K. Oppenheim Mason and A-M. Jensen (eds.), *Gender and Family Change in Industrialized Countries*. Oxford: Clarendon Press.

Lesthaeghe, R., and Surkyn, J. (1988). 'Cultural Dynamics and Economic Theories of Fertility Change.' *Population and Development Review* 14 (1): 1–45.

Lewis, J. (1984). *Women in England, 1870–1945*. Brighton: Harvester Wheatsheaf.

Lewis, J. (ed.). (1998). *Gender, Social Care and Welfare State Restructuring in Europe*. Aldershot: Ashgate.

Lewis, J. (1991). *Women and Social Action in Victorian and Edwardian England*. Cheltenham: Edward Elgar.

Lewis, J. (1992). 'Gender and the Development of Welfare Regimes.' *Journal of European Social Policy* 2 (3): 159–73.

Lewis, J. (1994). 'Gender, the Family and Women's Agency in the Building of "Welfare States": The British Case.' *Social History* 19(1): 38–55.

Lewis, J. (ed.). (1997). *Lone Mothers and European Welfare Regimes*. London: Jessica Kingsley.

Lewis, J. (1998). 'The Problem of Lone-Mother Families in Twentieth Century Britain.' *Journal of Social Welfare and Family Law* 20 (3): 251–84.

Lewis, J. (1999). 'New Labour, Nouvelle Grande-Bretagne? Les Politiques Sociales et la "Troisième Voie."' *Lien Social et Politiques* 41: 61–70.

Lewis, J. (2001). *The End of Marriage? Individualism and Intimate Relationships*. Cheltenham: Edward Elgar.

Lewis, J., and Astrom, G. (1992). 'Equality, Difference and State Welfare: Labour Market and Family Policies in Sweden.' *Feminist Studies* 18 (1): 59–87.

Lewis, J., Clark, D., and Morgan, D.H.J. (1992). *Whom God Hath Joined Together: The Work of Marriage Guidance*. London: Routledge.

Lewis, J., and Glennerster, H. (1996). *Implementing the New Community Care*. Buckingham: Open University Press.

Lindsey, B.B. and Evans, W. (1928). The *Companionate Marriage*. London: Brentano's Ltd.

Lister, R. (1997). *Feminism and Citizenship*. London: Macmillan.

Lister, R. (2000). 'Dilemmas of Pendulum Politics: Balancing Paid Work, Care and Citizenship.' Paper presented at the Conference on Re-inventing Feminism: Theory, Politics and Practice for the New Century, Goldsmiths College, London, May.

Luker, K. (1996). *Dubious Conceptions: The Politics of Teenage Pregnancy.* Cambridge, Mass: Harvard University Press.

Lundberg, S., and Pollak, R.A. (1996). 'Bargaining and Distribution in Marriage.' In I. Persson and C. Jonung (eds.), *Economics of the Family and Family Policies.* London: Routledge.

Lystra, K. (1989). *Searching the Heart: Women, Men and Romantic Love in Nineteenth Century* America. Oxford: Oxford University Press.

Macfarlane, A. (1986). *Marriage and Love in England, 1300–1840.* Oxford: Blackwell.

McIntosh, M. (1981). 'Feminism and Social Policy.' *Critical Social Policy* 1 (1): 32–42.

McLanahan, S. and Booth, K. (1989). 'Mother-Only Families: Problems, Prospects and Politics.' *Journal of Marriage and the Family* 51 (Aug.): 557–80.

Maclean, M. (1991). *Surviving Divorce. Women's Resources after Separation.* London: Macmillan.

Maclean, M. and Wadsworth, M.E.J. (1988). 'The Interests of Children after Parental Divorce: A Long Term Perspective.' *International Journal of Law and the Family* 2: 155–66.

McRae, S. (1993). *Cohabiting Mothers: Changing Mothers and Motherhood?* London: Policy Studies Institute.

McRae, S. (1997). 'Cohabitation: A Trial Run for Marriage?' *Sexual and Marital Theory* 12 (3): 259–73.

Manting, D. (1996). 'The Changing Meaning of Cohabitation and Marriage.' *European Sociological Review* 12 (1): 53–65.

Mead, L. (1986). *Beyond Entitlement: The Social Obligations of Citizenship.* New York: The Free Press.

Morgan, P. (1995). *Farewell to the Family: Public Policy and Family Breakdown in Britain and the USA.* London: IEA.

Mount, F. (1983). *The Subversive Family: An Alternative History of Love and Marriage.* London: Allen and Unwin.

Murphy, M. (2000). 'The Evolution of Cohabitation in Britain, 1960–95.' *Population Studies* 54: 43–56.

Murray, C. (1984). *Losing Ground: American Social Policy, 1950–1980.* New York: Basic Books.

Nelson, J.A. (1999). 'Of Markets and Martyrs: Is It OK to Pay Well for Care? *Feminist Economics* 4 (1): 43–59.

Newcomb, M.D. (1981). 'Heterosexual Cohabitation Relationships.' In S. Duck and R. Gilmour (eds.), *Personal Relationships: Studying Personal Relationships.* London: Academic Press.

Nock, S.L. (1995). 'A Comparison of Marriages and Cohabiting Relationships.' *Journal of Family Issues* 16 (1): 53–76.

Noddings, N. (1984). *Caring: A Feminist Approach to Ethics and Moral Education.* Berkeley: University of California Press.

Novak, M., and Cogan, J. (1987). *The New Consensus on Family and Welfare: A Community of Self-Reliance.* Milwaukee: American Enterprise Institute.

Nye, I.F. (1957). 'Child Adjustment in Broken and in Unhappy Unbroken Homes.' *Journal of Marriage and Family Living* 19: 356–61.

OECD. (1991). *Shaping Structural Change.* Paris: OECD

OECD. (2000). *Economic Studies*, no. 31, 2000/2. Paris: OELI).

ONS. (1998). *Living in Britain: Results from the 1996 General Household Survey*, London: The Stationery Office.

Oakley, A. (1974). *The Sociology of Housework.* Oxford: Martin Robertson.

Okin, S.M. (1989). *Justice, Gender and the Family.* New York: Basic Books.

Olsen, F.E. (1983). 'The Family and the Market: A Study of Ideology and Legal Reform.' *Harvard Law Review* 96 (7): 1497–578.

Oppenheim Mason, K., and Jensen, A-M (1995). 'Introduction.' In K. Oppenheim Mason and A-M. Jensen (eds.), *Gender and Family Change in Industrialized Countries.* Oxford: Clarendon Press.

Oppenheimer, V.K. (1994). 'Women's Rising Employment and the Future of the Family in Industrialised Societies.' *Population and Development Review* 20 (2): 293–342.

Pahl, R. (1996). 'Friendly Society.' In S. Kraemer, and J. Roberts (eds.). *The Politics of Attachment: Towards a Secure Society.* London: Free Association Books.

Pateman, C. (1988). *The Sexual Contract.* Cambridge: Polity Press.

Phillips, M. (1997). *The Sex Change State.* London: Social Market Foundation.

Phillips, R. (1988). *Putting Asunder: A History of Divorce in Western Society.* Cambridge: Cambridge University Press.

Phoenix, A. (1991). *Young Mothers.* Cambridge: Polity Press.

Piper, C. (1993). *The Responsible Parent. A Study in Divorce Mediation.* Brighton: Harvester Wheatsheaf.

Plantenga, J., Schippers, J., and Siegers, J. (1999). 'Towards an Equal Division of Paid and Unpaid Work: The Case of The Netherlands.' *Journal of European Social Policy* 9 (2): 99–100.

Popenoe, D. (1988). *Disturbing the Nest: Family Change and Decline in Modern Societies.* New York: Aldine de Gruyter.

Popenoe, D. (1993). 'American Family Decline, 1960–1990: A Review and Appraisal.' *Journal of Marriage and the Family* 55 (Aug.): 527–55.

Posner, R. (1992). *Sex and Reason.* Cambridge: Harvard University Press.

Prinz, C. (1995). *Cohabiting, Married or Single: Portraying, Analysing and Modelling New Living Arrangements in the Changing Societies of Europe.* Aldershot: Avebury.

Putnam, R.D. (1993). *Making Democracy Work: Civic Traditions in Modern Italy.* Princeton: Princeton University Press.

Regan, M.C. (1999). *Alone Together: Law and the Meanings of Marriage.* Oxford: Oxford University Press.

Richards, M.P.M., and Dyson, M. (1982). *Separation, Divorce and the Development of Children: A Review.* London: DHSS.

Riley, D. (1983). *War in the Nursery: Theories of the Child and the Mother.* London: Virago.

Rindfuss, R.R., and VandenHeuvel, A. (1990). 'Cohabitation: A Precursor to Marriage or an Alternative to Being Single?' *Population and Development Review* 16 (4): 703–26.

Rodgers, B., and Pryor, J. (1998). *Divorce and Separation: The Outcomes for Children.* York: Joseph Rowntree Foundation.

Rubery, J., Smith, M., and Fagan, C. (1998). 'National Working-Time Regimes and Equal Opportunities,' *Feminist Economics* 4 (1): 71–101.

Russell, B. (1929). *Marriage and Morals.* London: George Allen and Unwin.

Safilios Rothschild, C. (1970). 'The Study of Family Power Structure: A Review 1960–69.' *Journal of Marriage and the Family* 32 (4): 539–52.

Safilios Rothschild, C. (1976). 'A Macro- and Micro-Examination of Family Power and Love: An Exchange Model.' *Journal of Marriage and the Family* 38 (2): 355–62.

Sandel, M. (1982). *Liberalism and the Limits of Justice*. Cambridge: Cambridge University Press.

Sandel, M. (1996). *Democracy's Discontent: America in Search of a Public Philosophy*. Cambridge, Mass.: Belknap Press of Harvard University Press.

Schoen, R. (1992). 'First Unions and the Stability of First Marriage.' *Journal of Marriage and the Family* 54 (May): 281–4.

Schoen, R., and Weinick, R. (1993). 'Partner Choice in Marriages and Cohabitations.' *Journal of Marriage and the Family* 55 (May): 408–14.

Schultz, M. (1982). 'Contractual Ordering of Marriage: A New Model for State Policy.' *California Law Review* 70 (2): 204–334.

Scott, J. (1997). 'Changing Household in Britain: Do Families Matter?' *Sociological Review* 45 (4): 591–620.

Sen, A. (1987). *The Standard of Living: The Tanner Lectures*. Cambridge: Cambridge University Press.

Shorter, E. (1975). *The Making of the Modern Family*. London: Fontana.

Siim, B. (1987). 'The Scandinavian Welfare States – Towards Sexual Equality or a New Kind of Male Domination?' *Acta Sociologica* 30 (3/4): 255–70.

Singer, J. B. (1989). 'Divorce Reform and Gender Justice.' *North Carolina Law Review* 67 (5): 1103–121.

de Singly, F. (1996). *Modern Marriage and Its Loss to Women: A Sociological Look at Marriage in France*. London: Associated University Presses.

Sklar, K.K. (1995). *Florence Kelley and the Nation's Work: The Rise of Women's Political Culture, 1830–1900*. New Haven: Yale University Press.

Skocpol, T. (1991). *Protecting Soldiers and Mothers. The Political Origins of Social Policy in the US*. Cambridge, Mass.: Belknap Press of Harvard University Press.

Skocpol, T. (2000). *The Missing Middle: Working Families and the Future of American Social Policy*. New York: Norton.

Skolnick, A. (1991). *Embattled Paradise: The American Family in an Age of Uncertainty*. New York: Basic Books.

Smart, C., and Neale, B. (1997a). 'Wishful Thinking and Harmful Tinkering? Sociological Reflections on Family Policy.' *Journal of Social Policy* 26 (3): 301–21.

Smart, C., and Neale, B. (1997b). 'Good Enough Morality? Divorce and Postmodernity.' *Critical Social Policy* 53: 3–27.

Smart, C. and Neale, B. (1999). *Family Fragments*. Cambridge: Polity Press.

Smart, C. and Stevens, P. (2000). *Cohabitation Breakdown*. York: Joseph Rowntree Foundation.

Smith, B.A. (1990). 'The Partnership Theory of Marriage: A Borrowed Solution Fails.' *Texas Law Review* 68 (4): 689–743.

Smock, P.J., and Gupta, S. (2000). 'Cohabitation in Contemporary North America.' Paper given to the Family Issues Symposium, Population Research Institute, Pennsylvania State University.

Sorensen, A., and McLanahan, S. (1987). 'Married Women's Economic Dependency, 1940–1980.' *American Journal of Sociology* 93 (3): 659–87.

Spence, J.C. (1946). *The Purpose of the Family.* Convocation lecture for the National Children's Home. London: National Children's Home.

Spencer, H. (1876). *The Principles of Sociology* (Vol. 1). London: Williams and Norgate.

Stacey, J. (1990). *Brave New Families: Stories of Domestic Upheaval in Late Twentieth Century America*. New York: Basic Books.

Statistics Canada (1999). 'General Social Survey: Time Use.' In *The Daily*, 9 No., pp. 1–6.

Stone, L. (1979). *The Family, Sex and Marriage in England, 1500–1800*. Harmondsworth: Penguin.

Strathern, M. (1992). *After Nature: English Kinship in the Late Twentieth Century.* Cambridge: Cambridge University Press.

Supiot, A. (1999). *Au Delà de L'Emploi*. Paris: Flammarion.

Svenhuijsen, S. (1998). *Citizenship and the Ethics of Care*. London: Routledge.

Thair, T., and Risdon, A. (1999). 'Women in the Labour Market: Results from the Spring 1998 LFS,' *Labour Market Trends* (March), 103–27.

Thane, P. (1984). 'The Working Class and State "Welfare" in Britain, 1880–1914.' *Historical Journal* 27: 877–900.

Théry, I. (1994). *Le Demarriage*. Paris: Editions Odile Jacob.

Thomson, E., and Colella, U. (1992). 'Cohabitation and Marital Stability: Quality or Commitment?' *Journal of Marriage and the Family* 54: 259–67.

Tilly, L., and Scott, J. (1975). *Women, Work and Family.* New York: Holt Rinehart and Winston.

Titmuss, R.M. (1958). 'The Position of Women.' In R.M. Titmuss (ed.), *Essays on theWelfare State.* London: Allen and Unwin.

Tronto, J.C. (1993). *Moral Boundaries: A Political Argument for an Ethic of Care.* London: Routledge.

Van de Kaa, D.J. (1987). 'Europe's Second Demographic Transition.' *Population Bulletin* 42: 1–59.

Vandenbroucke, F. (1998). *Social Democracy, Globalization and Inequality.* London: IPPR.

Walby, S. (1997). *Gender Transformations.* London: Routledge.

Wallerstein, J.S., and Kelly, J.B. (1980). *Surviving the Breakup: How Children and Parents Cope with Divorce.* London: Grant McIntyre.

Weeks, J., Donovan, C., and Heaphy, B. (1999). 'Everyday Experiments: Narratives of Non-Heterosexual Relationships.' In B. Silva and C. Smart (eds.), *The New Family.* London: Sage.

Weitzman, L. (1981). *The Marriage Contract: Spouses, Lovers and the Law.* New York: Free Press.

Weitzman, L. (1985). *The Divorce Revolution.* New York: Free Press.

White, S. (2000). 'Social Rights and the Social Contract – Political Theory and the New Welfare Politics.' *British Journal of Political Science* 30: 507–32.

Williams, J. (1994). 'Is Couverture Dead? Beyond a New Theory of Alimony.' *The Georgetown Law Journal* 82 (7): 2227–90.

Wilson, E. (1977). *Women and the Welfare State.* London: Tavistock.

Wilson, J.Q. (1993). *The Moral Sense.* New York: Free Press.

Wilson, W.J. (1987). *The Truly Disadvantaged.* Chicago: University of Chicago Press.

Winnicott, D. (1957). *The Child and the Family: First Relationships.* Edited by Janet Hardenberg. London: Tavistock Press.

Wistow, G., et al. (1996). *Social Care Markets: Progress and Prospects.* Buckingham: Open University Press.

Wolfe, A. (1989). *Whose Keeper? Social Science and Moral Obligation.* Berkeley: University of California.

Women's Unit. (1999). *Women's Individual Income 1996/7.* London: Cabinet Office.

Young, I.M. (1995). 'Mothers, Citizenship and Independence: A Critique of Pure Family Values.' *Ethics* 105: 535–56.

Young, L. (1954). *Out of Wedlock.* New York: McGraw-Hill.

Young, M., and Wilmott, P. (1973). *The Symmetrical Family.* London: Routledge and Kegan Paul.

Yudkin, S., and Holme, A. (1963). *Working Mothers and Their Children.* London: Michael Joseph.

Zelig, K.C. (1993). 'Putting Responsibility Back into Marriage: Making a Case for Mandatory Prenuptials.' *University of Colorado Law Review* 64: 1223–45.

Index

THE JOANNE GOODMAN LECTURES

1976
C.P. Stacey, *Mackenzie King and the Atlantic Triangle* (Toronto: Macmillan of Canada 1976)

1977
Robin W. Winks, *the Relevance of Canadian History: U.S. and Imperial Perspectives* (Toronto: Macmillan 1979)

1978
Robert Rhodes James, 'Britain in Transition'

1979
Charles Ritchie, 'Diplomacy: The Changing Scene'

1980
Kenneth A. Lockridge, *Settlement and Unsettlement in Early America: The Crisis of Political Legitimacy before the Revolution* (New York: Cambridge University Press 1981)

1981
Geoffrey Best, *Honour Among Men and Nations: Transformations of an Idea* (Toronto: University of Toronto Press 1982)

1982
Carl Berger, *Science, God, and Nature in Victorian Canada* (Toronto: University of Toronto Press 1983)

1983
Alistair Horne, *The French Army and Politics, 1870–1970* (London: Macmillan 1984)

1984
William Freehling, 'Crisis United States Style: A Comparison of the American Revolutionary and Civil Wars'

1985
Desmond Morton, *Winning the Second Battle: Canadian Veterans and the Return to Civilian Life, 1915–1930* (published with Glenn Wright as joint author, Toronto: University of Toronto Press 1987)

1986
J.R. Lander, *The Limitations of the English Monarchy in the Later Middle Ages* (Toronto: University of Toronto Press 1989)

1987
Elizabeth Fox-Genovese, 'The Female Self in the Age of Bourgeois Individualism'

1988
J.L. Granatstein, *How Britain's Weakness Forced Canada into the Arms of the United States* (Toronto: University of Toronto Press 1989)

1989
Rosalind Mitchison, *Coping with Destitution: Poverty and Relief in Western Europe* (Toronto: University of Toronto Press 1991)

1990
Jill Kerr Conway, 'The Woman Citizen: Transatlantic Variations on a Nineteenth-Century Feminist Theme'

1991
P.B. Waite. *The Loner: Three Sketches of the Personal Life and Ideas of R.B. Bennett, 1870–1947* (Toronto: University of Toronto Press 1992)

1992
Christopher Andrew, 'The Secret Cold War: Intelligence Communities and the East-West Conflict'

1993
Daniel Kevles, 'Nature and Civilization: Environmentalism in the Frame of Time'

1994
Flora MacDonald, 'An Insider's Look at Canadian Foreign Policy Initiatives since 1957'

1995
Rodney Davenport, *Birth of a New South Africa* (Toronto: University of Toronto Press, 1997)

1996
Ged Martin, 'Past Futures: Locating Ourselves in Time'

1997
Donald Akenson, *If the Irish Ran the World: Montserrat, 1630–1730* (Montreal: McGill-Queen's University Press, 1997)

1998
Terry Copp, 'Fields of Fire: The Canadians in Normandy'

1999
T.C. Smout, 'The Scots at Home and Abroad, 1600–1750'

2000
Jack P. Greene, 'Speaking of Empire: Celebration and Disquiet in Metropolitan Analyses of the Eighteenth-Century British Empire'

2001

Jane E. Lewis, *Should We Worry about Family Change?*
(University of Toronto Press, 2003)

2002

Jacalyn Duffin, 'Lovers and Livers: Disease Concepts in History'